D0162778

Coercion and
Autonomy

Recent Titles in
Contributions in Philosophy

Coercion and Autonomy

PHILOSOPHICAL FOUNDATIONS, ISSUES, AND PRACTICES

ALAN S. ROSENBAUM

CONTRIBUTIONS IN PHILOSOPHY, NUMBER 31

GREENWOOD PRESS
NEW YORK • WESTPORT, CONNECTICUT • LONDON

HM271
R64
1986

Library of Congress Cataloging-in-Publication Data

Rosenbaum, Alan S.
 Coercion and autonomy.

 (Contributions in philosophy, ISSN 0084-926X ;
no. 31)
 Bibliography: p.
 Includes index.
 1. Authority. 2. Autonomy. 3. Power (Social
sciences) I. Title. II. Series.
HM271.R64 1986   303.3'6   86-7578
ISBN 0-313-22819-1 (lib. bdg. : alk. paper)

Copyright © 1986 by Alan S. Rosenbaum

All rights reserved. No portion of this book may be
reproduced, by any process or technique, without the
express written consent of the publisher.

Library of Congress Catalog Card Number: 86-7578
ISBN: 0-313-22819-1
ISSN: 0084-926X

First published in 1986

Greenwood Press, Inc.
88 Post Road West, Westport, Connecticut 06881

Printed in the United States of America

The paper used in this book complies with the
Permanent Paper Standard issued by the National
Information Standards Organization (Z39.48-1984).
10 9 8 7 6 5 4 3 2 1

This book is dedicated to my wife, Mary; to my children, Emily, Jascha, and Elizabeth; and to my teacher and friend, the late Professor Marvin Farber.

APR 2 7 1987

Contents

Acknowledgments

There are many persons who assisted me in a variety of ways in the preparation of this book. To them I owe a profound debt of gratitude. Some gave me encouragement, others critiqued portions of the manuscript, and still others readied it for submission to Greenwood Press.

My thanks are due to Professor Berkley Eddins (State University of New York at Buffalo) for reviewing my manuscript, and for delicately pointing out some of its more egregious deficiencies; to Professor Leslie Armour (University of Ottawa) for his constructive critique; to Professor Stanley Rosen (Penn State) for his words of encouragement; and finally to the professional consultants at Greenwood Press whose identities remain unknown to me but whose critique of my work has proven invaluable. Despite the careful reading others have given to my manuscript, errors of logic and judgment surely remain; blame for these must be placed solely at my doorstep.

I am indebted to James T. Sabin, Vice-President of Greenwood Press, and to his editorial staff, for their abiding belief in the worthiness of my work and for tolerating the endless inquiries and editorial exchanges needed to finish this book. My thanks to Cindy Bellinger for typing the various drafts of the manuscript, for computerizing it, and for eliminating the most obvious typographical and orthographical mistakes.

To my wife, Mary, I owe special thanks for enduring with seemingly boundless patience the continuous discussions I required in order to clarify and explain my thoughts and for proofreading everything I wrote. Her ever present love and understanding through all of this is given special note because she always manages to find the time and patience to help me, in addition to meeting the needs and demands of her own profession. The cooperation and love of my children, Emily Rose, Jascha William, and Elizabeth Ann, were a continuing source of strength without which the appearance of this book would have been delayed indefinitely. It is my hope that someday my children will read this book with a sense of pride and inspiration.

Preface

This book was written for professional philosophers, advanced students of philosophy, philosophically inclined practitioners in the allied fields of sociology, social psychology, politics and public policy, and law, and for the educated layperson. Its main focus is the conceptual relationship between human social autonomy and coercion.

Surprisingly, there is (to my knowledge) no other major book-length treatment of coercion in the recent philosophical literature, except for an edited volume of brief articles, that is directed specifically towards this realm of human relations. Though much has already been written in the professional journals of philosophy about coercion, the theory I develop in this volume is unique while it also manages to consider the theories presented in the writings of others.

My thesis is that 'coercion' is a relational and dynamic concept that is definable mainly with respect to relative and shifting spheres of human autonomy. Accordingly, the view I propose and seek to defend is the following: Q is coerced by P when P causes Q to relinquish his or her known and valued autonomy over him or herself in some limited respect.

Towards this end, the principal achievement of the book is the analysis of the concept of coercion given in Chapter 5. The foundation of this analysis is in the notions of autonomy, role, and intersubjective relationships that are defined and examined in the preceding chapters. Diagrams are included where suitable to visually represent what is involved in the relationships so described. The final chapter discusses the impact of ideology on a conception of coercion by surveying a variety of influential historical views of autonomy and coercion at different periods.

It is my hope that this work will contribute to a more refined philosophical understanding of coercion and in so doing to an avoidance of the ambiguities, inconsistencies, and mistaken judgments often associated with everyday practices and usages of 'coercion'.

Coercion and Autonomy

CHAPTER 1

Coercion in Theory
and Practice

It is my aim in this chapter to examine the various basic elements that constitute a concept of coercion. Contemporary writers on this subject often disagree on what should be included in a list of such elements. Even when some agreement is found on the inclusion of certain key elements, it is not uncommon for us to find disparate interpretations concerning the specific nature of the element or how it is conceived to function as applied to everyday situations. In any case, a selection will be made in the growing body of contemporary definitions of coercion from among those that exhibit the differences referred to about the elements of coercion. Accordingly, others' definitions will be used as a framework for introducing my own considerations about what an improved or good definition will require as a move towards a broader critique of contemporary philosophical accounts of coercion and its related ideas of general freedom and autonomy.

Implicit in this chapter is a fundamental recognition that the philosophical literature, present and past (as we shall show), abounds in studies of such important abstractions as human 'freedom', 'autonomy', 'privacy', and 'human rights'. In contrast, however, very little has been said philosophically about coercion itself as a philosophical notion, at least until recently. Yet, interferences with freedom, infringements on autonomy, invasions of privacy, and human rights violations often involve some kind of coercion and indeed these are sometimes understood as being various definitions of coercion. Since these abstractions are not synonymous with one another, to define coercion in terms of them is, then, to obscure any consistent meaning of coercion. In a certain sense, then, the history of the concept of coercion is coextensive with that of the abstractions mentioned above, but also it is probably viewed intuitively by most of us as a pejorative, normative concept owing, perhaps, to its close but negating relationship to freedom, autonomy, and so forth. The intuition is that the burden of justification is presumed to fall on the coercing agent while the victim is perceived as being largely responsibility-free for the actions done under coercion, the moral principle being that one is not to be held accountable for actions (done) over which one had no personal or direct control. Coercion is presumed to wrest all self-control over one's own actions. Though it is common, traditional, and perhaps reasonable, as it is done in philosophies of morality, politics, and law, to connect coercion with freedom and these other notional abstractions, it must be understood that this linkage renders the concept of coercion heir to many of the same obscurities and other difficulties engendered by similar weaknesses in the other notions.

SIGNIFICANCE OF COERCION

Two such encumbrances are readily noticeable. If there is an initial presumption in favor of, say, the abstract 'freedom of the individual', those persons or policies that interfere with an exercise of freedom are viewed *prima facie* as being in need of justification (i.e., there is an initial bias against such interference). One major difficulty that emerges upon consideration is found in the unhistorical fashion in which 'individual freedom' is conceived, as its many critics have suggested; the point being that the conditions of life, both natural and personal-social, belie any ascription of initial 'freedom' (e.g., X is free if X is left alone or a social policy of non-interference is X's best guarantee of freedom). Thus, coercion seems to acquire its normative meaning in this way. But another difficulty is soon apparent for, as we search out the roots of its normative significance, the concept of coercion may assume an ideological character owing to the initial bias of its presumed relationship to abstract notions of freedom (which themselves have been conceived along ideological lines).[1]

In recent years some writers have attempted nonnormative, purely descriptive, and value-neutral analyses of freedom, autonomy, privacy, and rights. Some others, though very few, have tried to do the same with 'coercion'. But the distinction between normative and nonnormative senses of freedom and coercion may be very difficult to maintain, especially if it overlooks ideological affinities or presuppositions. If, as its expositors claim, the non-normative view of coercion withholds judgment regarding its badness or goodness, wrongness or rightness, and seeks only to identify its key conditions, features, and elements, and prefers to leave to others any normative application, there is much in this approach that is of value for the present task. Specifically, it is by way of an examination of the basic elements of coercion that I will, in the main, attempt to clarify the concept of coercion and to suggest how intrusive ideological preconceptions may influence the outcome of how coercion is conceived and how its usage and consequences are to be assessed.

There are three preliminary assumptions upon which the following analysis proceeds. First, by *coercion* is meant certain forms of social control that are a subset of some types of exercises of power (between the participants in a power relationship). My focus is on power relationships both political and nonpolitical (e.g., interpersonal), insofar as coercion is an act and form of power. Other sorts of human relationships (i.e., non-power relationships) in which influence occurs or someone's freedom is limited by someone else but that are not inherently power-based in the restricted meaning given to the term 'power' here are beyond the range of immediate concern, such as love relationships, ritualistic exchanges, educational transactions, and so on. Another example is: a citizen of one country is subject to its laws and to his own country's authority's control over him, but he is ordinarily said to be beyond the reach of the civil laws of a country not his own. In this sense the citizen is independent of the legal authority of another country; each party is presumed to have no legal power relation with the other. If no power relation exists between the two parties, they are spoken of as being in that sense independent of each other— not independent necessarily of all influence and relatedness but only of influence involving power. A country may tax its own citizens without (power-based) interference from another country (under usual circumstances). In addition, nonhuman life forms and agents of causation are excluded from the present consideration of coercion (including such entities as other animals, mere physical, chemical, or material agencies, or purported 'spiritual' agencies) primarily because coercion is conceived solely as a social relationship of a certain kind among human beings.

Of course, it may be supposed that if other forms of life assume basic human qualities such as the possession of an autonomous will, a rational capacity, the ability to form intentions and to frame life-plans as well as the means to execute them, then any reason to exclude these entities from consideration as participants in a (coercive) social relationship would seem arbitrary. In brief, severe bad weather may compel us to change our vacation plans; a vicious dog may persuade a mail carrier to respect the wisdom of circumvention; chronic unemployment may prompt someone to steal food for his or her family's consumption; and a scarcity of available resources may force us to rethink our intention of sending our children to a high-priced academy. But these are ruled out in this analysis as coercing agents since they are (obviously) nonhuman and so are not possible participants in the relational configuration of coercion. These events are not to be regarded as instances of social coercion because they are not instances of power in the stipulated social sense.

The second assumption being made is that there are at least two universally recognized elements of coercion that are held to be basic or intrinsic: the *participants* in a coercive power relationship; and the *actions* of the participants. By 'participants' is meant the actors themselves, both the coercing agent (coercer) and the coercee or victim of coercion. By 'actions' I refer to the (victim's) 'action' done under coercion and/or the coercing agent's action that causes the coercee to perform the coerced action.

ON PARTICIPANTS

But something more is being supposed when 'participants' and 'actions' are identified as basic elements of coercion. Certainly, 'participants' are human beings, but how human beings are characterized (e.g., the nature of human nature, if there is one) remains both a perpetually puzzling philosophical matter and a potentially mischievous device of analysis if one set of descriptions of nature is preferred over some other set. For instance, are human beings basically rational and so inclined towards a peaceful existence, or are they aggressive and intrinsically emotional (irrational) and so predisposed towards a climate of struggle and domination? Or, both? And, of course, there are a number of other equally inviting possibilities. The most important implication of such descriptions, mainly for the analysis of coercion since it is based on the idea of the social interrelatedness of the participants in a coercive event, involves how the possibilities of interrelatedness are tied to the conception of the participants as human beings (i.e., the preferred set of descriptions). For example, if the conception of self-identity is essentially and thoroughly social, the idea of personal privacy as a dominant value represents alienation from one's own nature and perhaps a form of social defiance and malady. For coercion in this context, then, as an invasion of 'privacy' would be no invasion at all since the realm of privacy supposedly invaded is neither inviolable in the moral sense nor is respect for it a prerequisite of human health or the well-being of society.

There is a danger that an analysis of coercion, like that of freedom, may become implicitly ideological unless the nature of participants is explicitly dealt with: is the participant construed as a person who assumes the character of the abstract individual (of classical liberal theory), the social individual (of social liberalism), or the 'community' human (of Soviet Marxism, Chinese Communism, African Tribalism)? In each of these cases a certain set of possible relations is posited that is very different from those of the others, as the self-identity example above is meant to suggest. Another example that comes readily to mind involves various forms of (institutional, personal; political and legal) racism. If the 'racist' class arrogates to itself the basic human qualities it denies to the 'inferior' class such as fundamental human rights and personal moral autonomy, coercion against members of the inferior class cannot be described as violating rights since there are supposedly none to violate. It might be objected that coercion need not be defined solely in terms of certain rights violations; then, from the racist's viewpoint, it could be claimed that none of the distinctive qualities that constitute 'humanity' are present at least to the same extent in other 'inferior' life forms. And so coercion that may be construed in terms of (assaults against) qualities like autonomy, rationality, choice-making capacity, and so forth, would be no more conceivable against members of an inferior class than against, say, a dog or cat. Dogs and cats are often forced to do some things they do not appear inclined to do on their own, but for good reasons we do not usually describe such actions as coercion: 'use of force' does not always, or even mainly, signify coercion, nor does coercion always involve use of force. The nature, forms, and range of possible relations between 'participants', then, is a conceptual product of how 'participants' are (to be) understood.

ACTION

The use of the term 'action' is also in need of additional comment. It is crucial for an understanding of coercion relations because these invariably involve certain classes of actions. Actions may be voluntary, habitual, deliberate or impulsive, but not all forms of human behavior are actions or 'action' movements. Reflex movements (like eye-blinking or muscle tics) and other involuntary forms of behavior (like screaming when abruptly frightened, slipping on icy pavement, or being pushed or dragged around) should not be classified as actions because they lack the element of choice, which is the defining feature of 'action' as the term is used here. In general whenever a participant agent, Q, performs some action, q, in order for 'choice' to have informed this behavior, at least one alternative action must have existed or have been available: not doing q, which it is/was possible to perform or not perform under the circumstances at the moment. Choosing not to do q also counts as an action even though it is behavior by omission. Though the normal course of events for reflex movements like eye-blinking is involuntary, we may on purpose interrupt such from time to time. Indeed, such acts of omission—negative actions—are at least as common in everyday personal as well as legal, political, and moral affairs. For instance, I may elect not to forward my yearly dues to the APA this year; or, the U.S. government may make it punishable for school boards to approve the practice of requiring prayers in its public schools: 'refusing to approve' constitutes a negative action. Finally, 'action' is meant to be limited only to those processes of consciousness (will, intentions) resulting in some form of choice-made behavior (irrespective of unintended consequences). In brief, q is an action of Q when and only when q is causally linked to Q's choice to perform q. Needs, desires, beliefs, and interests are four sorts of reasons that specific choices are made and actions taken.

There is a third assumption that is implied by the first (that coercion is a kind of social power relation): the coercive relationship involves more than two terms. The following are typical of two-term definitions: the victim and the victim's (coerced) action or, perhaps, the victim and his unwilling compliance with something unwanted. Others that include two participants usually include a third element: an action, will, consent, and/or intention. Hence, contemporary definitions of coercion that fail to consider the social nature of the event, including the source, the participants, the condition(s), the instruments, and the specific nature of the coercion in some given situation, should be regarded as inadequate. Because someone has been compelled to act against his will does not *ipso facto* make one a victim of coercion, as suggested earlier by non-social power influences on behavior.

There are a number of other troubling situations, however, that command a reexamination of the whole notion of coercion, for a fuller account needs to be given of its basic conceptual elements. It is not sufficient that the following common or increasingly common range of situations be shunted off as borderline cases of coercion, or else dismissed as irrelevant or trivial, or, on the other hand, as intuitively obvious. What is obvious is that the complexity of some of the situations adduced below points up the evident inadequacy of two-term definitions of coercion.

Two-term definitions are distinguished from three- (or more) term definitions hereafter called 'relational' definitions because they include the relationship between at least two participants and their actions.

Perhaps the most dramatic of the situations selected was reported in a newspaper article.[2] Presumably the author of the article spelled out most of the relevant facts of the case, so readers will be spared a rehash now. In brief, a cancer victim, William Head, twenty-six years old, has been told by his physicians that he has about six months to live unless he receives a bone marrow transplant. "The procedure, which is highly experimental when it involves donations by someone other than a twin or close relative, has only a small chance of success. For the donor of healthy marrow, there is little risk to life. There is, however, considerable discomfort." A computer search by a physician's assistant at the University Hospitals in Iowa City, Iowa, turned up the name of a California woman (Ms. X) whose tissue type seemed to match his, though she never offered to be classified as a potential donor of bone marrow, her name having appeared in the tissue-typing registry of the hospital for other reasons. The woman was contacted at Head's urgent request. She clearly indicated her unwillingness to become a donor. Head asked the university hospital staff to inform her of his plight and appeal to her again to be a donor. They denied his request on the ground that another appeal to Ms. X would be "unduly coercive." Mr. Head filed suit in court against the university staff's decision hoping to compel one more effort. The court ordered the hospital to inform Ms. X "that she is the only known donor who can help Head." In reversing the lower court ruling, the Iowa Supreme Court (3/28/83) rejected Head's request to notify Ms. X that she may be able to save his life. The court held that hospital records are confidential, and a dying leukemia victim's plight does not overrule that fact.

Suppose, on the one hand, it is claimed that Head has a basic right to life and a strong interest in acquiring the (potential) means to sustain him. And suppose Ms. X, on the other hand, has an inviolable right to privacy, "to be let alone," as a basic, universal democratic right. The compelling nature of both claims shows how this case raises many different moral issues concerning personal privacy, obligations to help others in our community, and so on. Nevertheless, only two sets of issues are singled out for present purposes because they help exemplify the inadequacy of the (nonrelational or nonsocial) two-term approach to defining coercion.

Take any two terms, for example, two participants, or a participant and his action, or the coercing action and the victim's (coerced) action (or contrary will), or a violation of someone's basic right, and so on. Apply each of these two-term approaches to both of the following sets of issues: (1) Is Ms. X a victim of coercion *because* she was approached by the University of Iowa Hospital staff in violation of her right to privacy? Would it be "unduly coercive" to do so again? (2) If we grant that everyone has some moral obligation for the well-being of others in his community (family, friends, strangers), do officials at the University Hospital have a moral obligation to grant Head's request? Does Ms. X have an obligation to listen again to, if not to grant, Head's appeal?

These two issues, regardless of whether their resolutions are affirmatively or negatively answered,[3] must appeal to other considerations besides merely identifying the factual presence of the two elements of (the two-term definition of) coercion in a given situation. It is not sufficient, for instance, to ask whether (in summary of the two sets of issues) the existence of a moral rule (concerning rights and obligations) lessens or negates the coerciveness of efforts to respect it or whether violations of it increase or constitute the essence of coercion? For these may and sometimes do count in our everyday calculations about whether or not someone has been coerced, but it counts as only one factor in deciding if coercion exists, important as it may be in some scheme of justification.

In the issues above it seems we also need to know, for instance, whether certain types of interaction (as in issue 1) are covered by the preferred 'privacy' doctrine; whether this doctrine is of supreme value over other fundamental moral and/or nonmoral doctrines and so disvalue always attaches to its breach? What means are used to accomplish the so-called coercion? It is not being suggested that the application of the term 'coercion' is prohibitive owing to an inexhaustible number of factors that must always be considered. Rather it is claimed that two-term definitions leave out of consideration too many basic factors that are commonly included in everyday judgments of coercion.

In general it will be useful to suggest a series of other, less dramatic issues in which application of the term 'coercion' is uncommon. However, the more peripheral nature of such issues, in regards to the term 'usual application', may allow us to observe more carefully the deficiency of two-term definitions, that is, for example, the mere fact that Q is compelled to act against his or her will does not *ipso facto* alone make him or her a victim of coercion. The two terms: (1) one's *action* taken (2) *against* one's will. One reason we cited was that coercion is an interpersonal or social relation. Thus a nonhuman agency like inclement weather may compel Y to change plans quite against his or her will. It also commends a reexamination of the whole notion of coercion, including a probe of what its basic elements are, for the following situations prompt issues that are not ostensibly dismissible as borderline cases, irrelevant or trivial.

(a) Has a patron been coerced for having yielded, quite against his or her will, to the restaurant's dress code in order to gain admittance? (Can entertainment activities be coercive?); Is feeling coerced the same as 'being coerced'? (b) Is peacetime military registration, required by law, a coercive form of government? (Would real threats to national security lessen the apparent coercive nature of the draft registration? Is national self-defense coercive? Is this a coercive form of unfreedom?); (c) Has a child been coerced when a parent compels him or her to eat only a nonsugared breakfast cereal for his or her own good (to prevent hyperactivity, dental caries, and so forth? How about if *not* for the child's own good? Does consideration of the consequences [detriment, well-being, and so on] affect the coerciveness of an act? Is paternalism coercive?); (d) Has a vicious-looking canine conceivably coerced the postal carrier into not delivering someone's (presumably his owner's) mail? (Can nonhuman lifeforms like animals coerce human beings?); (e) Has a football player whose opponent tackles him and so prevents him from achieving his 'touchdown' goal been coerced? (In their normal course, are competitive sports like football coercive?); and finally (f) has a person been coerced when forcibly or even nonviolently restrained from murdering someone? (Is the prevention of serious crime in this case coercion?) In all of the above situations there is a strong customary if not intuitive inclination by many *not* to label them instances of coercion; or else, if coercion, then they are seen as clearly justifiable or acceptable so as to transmute the coerciveness of their character and, in effect, to blind us to it. We shall return to these after benefit of the analysis of coercion that follows.

The three assumptions[4] described in the foregoing discussion provide a basis for the recognition of at least two other elements as fundamental to a definition and better understanding of coercion and its relatedness to abstractions like freedom, autonomy, privacy, and human rights.

INSTRUMENTS OF COERCION

Coercion is accomplished by the application of some instrument or means in many cases sufficient for its purpose. But the instruments of coercion are not necessarily physical objects (including someone's use of body strength) because participants may also be coercively controlled using nonphysical means such as threats (that are taken seriously). Despite the axiomatic character of the distinction between coercive actions and the instruments used to bring them about, we should be alert to a common error made by many (but by no means all) writers: the means by which coercion is accomplished—its instrument(s), such as physical force—is mistakenly interpreted as the definition of coercion, which, of course, it is not.

An untenable result of defining coercion as the application of physical force is that we are, then, compelled to regard as something other than coercion the more subtle relations of influence and control between participants. Accordingly, if physical force is only one kind of coercing instrument, we may suppose others exist such as threats, (coercive) offers, irresistible incentives, and so on. Finally it is also true that not all instances of physical force involve coercion. To show this we will have to distinguish between the following instances of physical force: (1) a wind sufficiently strong to push someone off a sidewalk, (2) a hoodlum abruptly pushing someone off a sidewalk, (3) the physical removal by police of a nonviolent anti-nuclear power protester from the tracks of an oncoming train believed to be transporting nuclear weapons, and (4) the protester (in case 3) who resists being removed from the tracks but is removed in spite of active resistance. The first instance involves a natural not social set of events; the second is a movement-causing act of physical violence, it is not coercion; it involves the victim's movement and not his or her action; the third is a noncoercive use of force by police despite the protester's obvious desire not to be removed. Unless the protester performs or attempts to perform some action as in instance 4, he or she is moved but not coerced. In instance 4 his or her futile active resistance involves an action of his or hers that is being prevented by the use of someone else's physical force. His or her removal from the train tracks is an action done under coercion. Again, physical force is not always coercive, and not all coercive events involve the application of physical force. Yet all coercive relations result from the use of some instrument, and so a fuller account of the concept of coercion must include 'instruments' as one of its basic elements.

SOCIAL ROLE

The other or second element, which to my knowledge has not been recognized by writers on the subject of coercion but should be included as an important element, is social 'role' or the 'role perspective'. Sociologists generally regard the 'role' phenomenon in social relationships as the basic unit of social analysis.[5]

In our analysis of the power-based social relationship (among the participants) in a coercive event, certain relevant factors or considerations appear that are not always obvious but that must be classified in some manner. The concept of role can be seen to subsume such considerations, and for this reason the 'role' perspective is included as a fourth element in a prospective definition of social coercion.

THE IDEOLOGICAL 'INDIVIDUAL'

Consideration of the often-implicit notion of the individual who acts as a participant (coercer or coercee) in a purportedly coercive event is one factor that the role perspective may reveal. Ideological bias may be crucial in determining whether a given action is to be counted as an instance of coercion inasmuch as differing ideologies may be reflected in differing conceptions of personhood.[6]

SPHERES OF AUTONOMY

Another factor that the role perspective classifies under its heading is the nature of the participants *as seen from an inter-subjective viewpoint*. This viewpoint on the nature of the participants is disclosed by the role perspective in the sense that the role perspective assists us in identifying encroachments on the 'spheres of autonomy' presumed to encircle each participant in a power relationship. Social coercion may be defined as a certain species of such encroachments. In this regard, though, I must state that I have no intention of aligning my concept and analysis of coercion with any explicit particular ideology.

It should be noticed that many writers, especially in the tradition of Western liberal theory, have attributed inherent 'spheres of autonomy' to specific individual human beings *qua* human nature. It is a common presumption among many such writers to regard human beings as such as autonomous in virtue of their inherent rational agency. Accordingly it is conceivable, then, if we follow in this tradition, to attribute to any participant in a coercive relationship *qua* human being, that is, separate from any situation-dependent qualifications, an a priori, fixed sphere of autonomy. To the contrary, I acknowledge a relational view of human autonomy, that spheres of autonomy attributable to human beings involved in (coercive) social relationships may vary with those relationships. Hence, a key factor in an analysis of coercion concerns the spheres of autonomy of the various participants in a specific power relation *relative to each other* (as well as an assessment of the type of situation with respect—ultimately—to basic human needs, desires and satisfactions, interest, and perhaps rights and freedoms).

Although 'roles' are usually regarded as an objective sociological category and social phenomenon, the fact is they also have or may be given intersubjective significance. The intersubjective reference to social role contributes something to an analysis of coercion that seems unavailable from an objective, empirical perspective. Hence, the third factor the role perspective is meant to subsume is the nature of the *relationship* between participants in a coercive event. The way in which the participants themselves understand their relationship(s) is an important factor, as revealed by a role perspective, in determining whether a given social action, event, and relationship is coercive. *Intersubjectivity* is the term that will refer to this manner of understanding among participants: it is inherent in any human interaction, but it is not always objectively given. Further, the notion of intersubjectivity includes not only face-to-face coercive relations but also coercive power or control relations exercised indirectly, through others, and at a distance. On balance it is also true that social roles may in specific cases have an objective side and often, only an objective definition.

CONCLUDING REMARKS

How the participants in a coercive power-based role relationship have been characterized has implications for interpreting the other two elements mentioned, actions and instruments. Coercive relationships, like other forms of interpersonal and political relations, can usually be seen to presuppose a certain set of features concerning the nature of the participants as conceived, however implicitly, in a given relationship. It becomes evident that these interpreted features share an uncritical bias or conceptual affinity to classical Western liberal individualism. Therefore, a significant number of recent philosophical works dealing with an analysis of coercion become implicitly, and sometimes explicitly, ideological. Ideological bias of this sort may be decisive in determining whether some action or relationship is an instance of coercion, because it sets the terms in which coercion and its elements are defined. Cases of this bias may express perfectly acceptable usage within the framework of liberalism (or any preferred ideology), but when an analysis of coercion is framed in such terms, its significance and value as a nonnormative or scientific 'value free' concept, which many writers believe it is, must then be questioned. Whether or not there are nonideological notions of normativeness with regards to the concept of coercion remains to be discussed.

PROCEDURAL TERMINOLOGY DEFINED

Coercion is a complex term as an analysis of its key features will reveal. To identify and properly place these features, some standardization of our vocabulary is necessary since the meanings of the following terms serve as our tools of analysis. The *elements* of coercion refer both to any fundamental or principle part of the conception or to any factor that is indispensable to determining coercion. An example would be someone's unsuccessful resistance to someone else's effort to shove him or her off the sidewalk. An important factor is the successful action (pushing) of the coercer.

The term 'action' becomes an element in the analysis of coercion inasmuch as coercion always involves some participant's action (viz., the coercer's or coercee's).

A distinctive quality or characteristic of the concept is its *feature*. A main feature of a coercive relation is the coerced action of a victim. An act of coercion is by definition always successful so whatever is necessary for it becomes a *condition* of its success. For instance, reluctant submission to someone else's action or threat to take coercive action may count as a condition of coercion when taken for that reason alone, if without the other's action or threat the victim would likely have done otherwise.

Once we have identified the elements of coercion, it becomes possible to form judgments about what sorts of relations and events are coercive. Taken together or in some special combination, these elements constitute a standard or *criterion* for applying the term 'coercion' to a variety of situations. There are different *types* of coercion: one type may use physical violence as an instrument to accomplish the purpose of the coercing agent; another might use some persuasive threat. Even though the resulting action of the victim might be the same in either case, the use of violence may be regarded as a key feature of one type of coercion, namely, those relations that are characterized by such violence, as distinguished from coercive relations effected by the use of threats. Further, coercion is generally thought to be a type of action apart from others. An *instance* of coercion is merely an example or specific case of a coercive relation that may be cited in defense or elaboration of a general statement about coercion involving its elements.

There are *degrees* of coercion. For example, there is a greater measure of coercion when someone is forcibly restrained from reaching a highly desired goal than if the goal being pursued is relatively undesirable ('he didn't really want to do it anyway'). Restraining a person from accidentally walking into the path of an oncoming vehicle is not ordinarily thought of as coercive in any degree. It is also true that 'degree' of coercion may be determined by other factors besides value priorities, such as the mere fact of someone's interference in someone else's behavior, or the situation itself, or the means used to coerce (some subtle and not so subtle techniques of influence and control [e.g., psychosurgery, the political use of psychiatry, etc.] are nonetheless coercive).

This analysis of coercion, as well as others', is aided by a distinction between the variables and constants in the various concepts of coercion. A 'variable' refers to a factor or quantity that changes or varies, for example, threats may vary in type from situation to situation, just as the instruments of coercion may (viz., those things by means of which coercion is done). (Coercion itself is instrumentalized when it is utilized for certain purposes, but, in this case, the instrumentaliztion of coercion nevertheless presupposes the same sorts of elements that make it the coercive tool that other tools are when used to coerce.) Anything in the conception of coercion that is uniform in value or unchanging in value, nature, or degree is called a 'constant'. Accordingly, I construe participants and actions as constants in my view of coercion, though an overview of the philosophical literature will regard these as variables because their nature has been interpreted differently from writer to writer, or at least among those who accept these as basic elements, which some do not.

Ultimately this work is intended to contribute to an improved definition of coercion. By *definition* is meant an explication that purports to reduce the vagueness of the ordinary, or intuitive, notion of coercion. The present efforts at reconstruction are aimed at clarifying the meaning of coercion and so enabling us to distinguish between certain social contexts of coercion: the inter-personal and the political, while not reducing the latter to the former through subtle ideological presupposition. Secondarily, the aim is to impose a classification scheme upon diverse contemporary treatments of coercion. In the following section references to 'legal theory' are not to be understood merely as shadows of the positive legal order; moral theory is not merely a reflection of any specific personal or cultural bias or practice; nor is 'political theory' meant as reducible to political science.

APPENDICES TO CHAPTER 1

A. CONCEPTS OF COERCION IN LAW, POLITICS, AND ETHICS

The following examples have been chosen for discussion due to the clarity with which they express the concept of coercion.

1. In Law

The concepts of coercion and law (particularly Anglo-American law) intersect at any number of places: in criminal law, in tort and contract law, and in constitutional law. For example, in criminal law, robbery (see Model Penal Code 222.1) and rape (see Model Penal Code 213.1) are offenses that are defined in terms of coercion or involve coercion in some of its forms. Legal prohibitions against these offenses go to the heart of the rules that make it possible for society itself to exist: they are meant to protect personal safety and security of property. In addition, some criminal acts are themselves labelled 'criminal' *because* they are coercive. "A person is guilty of criminal coercion if, with purpose to unlawfully restrict another's freedom of action to his detriment, he threatens to: (a) commit a criminal offense; or (b) accuse anyone of a criminal offense," (see Model Penal Code 212.5), and so on.

When giving consideration to coercion as a possible reasonable and affirmative defense in criminal law, it is clear that in the eyes of the law coercion has a normative character: it is used as a pejorative and condemnatory term. But whether or not rapists and murderers can use as a possible defense that they were coerced into rape and murder, and so claim to be excused in part or in whole, is a matter of continuing serious debate among legal scholars. Positions range from the "no recognition of excuses" view.[7]

In contract and tort law, coercion, duress, and undue influence are cited as possible defenses, depending upon conditions as defined by law. But when coercion has legal effect, it may be used illegally or give effect to an illegal act, or it may be a foregoing condition making an otherwise legal arrangement or action null, void, and so on. Even more generally an agreement involving coercion may be declared void if it "seriously offends law or public policy."[8]

Black's Law Dictionary defines coercion as follows: it "may be actual, direct, or positive, as where physical force is used to compel an act against one's will, or implied, legal or constructive, as where one party is constrained by subjugation to the other to do what his free will would refuse."[9]

There is an obvious overall legal bias against coercion that arises, no doubt, from certain philosophical, political, or moral presuppositions in the formation of a body of law, all involving in one essential way or another the sanctity of what is variously called 'privacy', 'autonomy', or 'personhood'. As a noted authority on the constitutional law observes: "In our day the [Supreme Court] justices have newly recognized the 'right to privacy'. . . . To date, at least, the right has brought little new protection for what most of us think of as 'privacy'—freedom from official intrusion. What the Supreme Court has given us, rather, is something essentially different and farther reaching, an additional zone of autonomy, of presumptive immunity to government regulation."[10] This distinction between 'public' and 'private' may be viewed as a product of a modern ideological conception of social relations.

Each of the concepts of coercion as it functions in the above-mentioned areas of law contains normative features, for example, a coercee may be excused from actions done under coercion since it is claimed that he had little or no control over the actions done, it may be a defense against wrongdoing; it may offend 'public policy'; it obstructs the expression of one's 'free will'; it may mean 'official intrusion'; and so on. The nonnormative features include constraints against performance; unwilling compliance effected by use of force; or "an intentional restriction of someone's freedom of action to his detriment," which has features of both. The contextual applications of the latter features in law imply a normative bias against coercion in the most general sense that law has as two of its prime purposes the safeguarding of life, liberty, and property, and the promotion of social stability and integration. Finally, in law, coercion is treated as having a certain set of elements that is basic to its conception. However, it is for purposes of convenience and classification that the normative/nonnormative categories are used. Generally, participants, actions, and instruments are all recognized in various degrees by the legal views of coercion mentioned above.

2. In Morality and Philosophical Ethics

A great many moral or ethical theorists today discuss the age-old problem: "What is the rational basis for acting as if human life has a peculiar value, quite beyond the value of any other natural things, when one can understand so clearly how different peoples for quite different reasons, have come to believe that it has a particular value and to affirm this in their different moralities?''[11] For instance, human rights theorists encounter this problem in their efforts to provide a rational basis for the foundation, nature, and variety of human rights claims.

In general morality has as its ultimate purpose the formulation of those minimum necessities and conditions that any person as a member of the human community needs to live a meaningful, dignified, and good life. Moreover, ethical theories aspire to provide a definitive basis for distinguishing right actions from wrong ones, good from bad. The normativeness of certain ethical principles and concepts is expressed as they recommend one action or set of actions over some other incompatible one. Failure to respect ethical prescriptions, it is commonly held, places the community at the risk of destroying the possibility of living 'the good life'.

Points of intersection between ethics and coercion can be identified from the standpoint of one or the other of two of the most prominent ethical theories that many human rights theories have as their basis, namely, (J. S. Mill's) utilitarianism and (Kant's) ethical formalism.

Utilitarians tend to deny the autonomy of ethics claiming instead that, for instance, individual liberty may rightly be restricted for the sake of some more important benefit like the prevention of harm or suffering. In any case moral rights are never conceived by utilitarians as being inviolable if Mill's philosophy is representative. The particular nature of the consequences of some action receive the weightiest consideration.

Formalist ethics like Kant's, on the other hand, is grounded on a conception of the human being as a rational, autonomous being in virtue of his or her 'humanity'. However, it is his metaphysics of morality and not the specific doctrine of 'being human' ''that fashions the compelling moral virtue and obligations which constitute moral excellence.''[12] It is duty for the sake of duty and not for some supposed beneficial result that is a major distinguishing mark between formalism and utilitarianism.

In a Kantian view, ''freedom is understood as independence from the arbitrary coercion of another,'' and this Kant understands as the most basic, irreducible human right.[13] This is not an unconditional rejection of coercion, as it seems to suggest, but rather a *prima facie* or relative rejection. The possession of a basic right also gives the title-holder a 'title to compel' respect for the right in question. Nevertheless, it is the formalist who comes closer than the utilitarian in giving coercion a basically negative or highly disvaluable status in the principles of morality.

The utilitarian, on the other hand, may be disposed initially to reject coercion as evil, owing to its invasive delimitations of personal freedom. But he or she is even more inclined, despite Mill's thesis in *On Liberty* to the contrary, to find some justification for coercive practices inasmuch as no moral principle is sufficiently supreme or absolute. Built-in doctrinal constraints are simply not as available to the utilitarian as to the formalist. For example, if human rights are established on utilitarian grounds for the sake of utility, they can be outweighed by other considerations.

In any case both normative and nonnormative features are observable in the theories mentioned, each theory purporting to describe the individual as a moral agent yet prescribing the types of behaviors and motives most befitting its respective conception. Insofar as ethical or moral principles are conceived as rules for any of these prescriptions, I view moral theories as ultimately normative in character; they are structured normatively to accomplish their purpose. The elements of coercion are typically participants and actions, for proponents of these theories apparently consider its instruments as secondary, if relevant at all, to whatever constitutes coercion (much like N.R.A. spokespersons claiming "guns don't kill: people do," as if the instrument were absolutely separable from those who would use it).

For moral theories of this kind, as for both law and political theory, the practical question remains about the weight specific rights are to be accorded in balance against other things such as the public good and the appropriate method for limits in the enforcement of rights and their corresponding obligations.

3. In Political Theory

Views about what the ideal society is and how best to bring it about have long figured in the writings of history's foremost philosophers. From the classical Greeks and perhaps before them in the socioreligious doctrines of ancient Semitic tribes, to modern-day theorists of democracy, anarchy, communism, and their proliferating varieties and admixtures, the notion of coercion has found a near-central place. Either it is as a *bête noir* in doctrines of righteousness, goodness, rationality, happiness or justice[14] (it holds a strong bias against coercion), or it is accepted as an unavoidable necessity in theories of efficient political organization, especially in heavily populated societies and in theories of social dissensus, conflict, disintegration, and change. For example, Ralf Dahrendorf has claimed that "every society is based on the coercion of some of its members by others."[15] Coercion has even been touted as a positive historical force, for instance, in Jean Jacques Rousseau's notion of "forcing people to be free," in modern revolutionary struggles against the existing regimes provided that the opposition to revolution realizes that "violence is not a means of resisting the irresistible"[16] or in totalitarian ideologies like Nazism.

Political theorists are presumed to be inclined against coercion as an instrument of will, as most of us supposedly are, especially if noncoercive means are believed equally effective. In short, very few people are apostles of coercion whereas many are apostles of freedom and of authority (which some mistakenly view as coercion). In any case, coercion is generally regarded as a necessary evil in some situations, or as necessary to suppress elements of evil. This negative consideration is due to coercion's freedom-diminishing aspect. But the conception and specific value or warrant attached to coercion can be seen to hinge on how writers in political philosophy solve another broader difficulty.

A real problem has emerged in recent years for philosophers and political scientists in the split that has occurred between traditional political theories and some modern theories about political organization. This split involves the distinction between normative and nonnormative political theories, particularly those which discuss the notions of freedom and coercion. The key question concerning this split has been asked in the following way: what is the nature of political philosophy and its supposed relationship to contemporary political science? In brief, are past political theories, from Plato's to Marcuse's, merely normative, value-laden exercises in prescientific speculation?; and, is contemporary political science, on the

other hand, a nonnormative, value-neutral discipline dealing
primarily with empirical facts and predictions based on facts?[17]

It is true enough that the idea of political theory as a project
towards the formulation of a set of value statements and prescriptions about the ideal society has been seriously called into question,
but the ramifications of this dichotomy are seen in the task before
us now of trying to identify the character (normative, nonnormative) of certain elements concerning coercion that constitute many
contemporary political theories.

Certainly it is not as easy as it may first appear to separate
normative from nonnormative (fact from value) concepts and
ideas, in spite of the influence of positivism on both philosophy
and political science, for the difficulty is especially evident in
categorizing coercion-related notions like 'consent', 'rights',
'privacy', and 'freedom'. Sometimes coercion is treated explicitly
as an ethical category (e.g., it is held to be unqualifiedly evil); at
other times, it is not all that clear. Someone's unwilling compliance
to someone else's demands may seem purely descriptive, but a
closer look suggests the following: it is a basic good to exercise
one's own will unhampered by others, so to be prevented from
doing so is *bad*; or, a criminal must be compelled to obey or to
receive penalty; in either case coercion is *good*. Nevertheless these
categories of classification will be used with a serious qualification:
they are to be understood as methodological categories for the
limited purpose of classifying how certain elements function in an
analysis of coercion. No claim is being made, nor is it necessary to
do so about the scientific nature and value of this distinction or
for the results from making it, except to acknowledge that some
writers identify their conceptions of coercion as either normative or
nonnormative as the case may be.

The normative/nonnormative distinction applies to the points of
intersection between coercion and many political theories about
society. Examples can be found in both the classical and modern
literature. In each of the three instances selected—Plato's
Republic, Rawls' Liberal Democracy, and Marx's Communist
Society—the respective conceptions of social relations and humanity
underlay the attributions made about, in these cases, the normative
characters of its leading political principles with regards to how
coercion is or might be understood.

For the classical Greek philosopher Plato, there is no ultimate difference between what the principles of justice would require if understood from the viewpoint of the state or, on the other side, of the individual or citizen. For him or her the state is conceived as "man *writ large*" so what the 'essentials' of justice are remain the same in both cases. The conduct and policies pursued in proper fulfillment of the human soul parallels and contributes to the *politeia* ("soul of the polis"). Plato would not, it appears, be against all forms of coercion, nor does he consider "freedom of the individual" (e.g., against a supposed interference by the state) the dominant human value—as some modern theories do—for both are conceived and finally assessed on the basis of the soul's proper function. It is not the denial of freedom but of justice that is central to Plato's normative idea of coercion if coercion is understood as a form of disorder between citizens or between the state and its citizens.[18]

Liberal and social democracy is a denomination for a whole host of modern theories concerning the type of sociopolitical organization in which citizens are presumed to hold ultimate title over political processes and policy decisions that affect them. In John Rawls' modern contractarian theory of social democracy, the conception of social relations, as well as the moral principles to guide them, are a conceptual product of the common belief that justice imposes certain universal constraints upon everyone alike and that these must be decided upon in their particulars and also enforced by the citizenry at large for the resulting political power to be legitimate as well as just in its exercise.

For present purposes we may overlook the numerous complex concepts and methods used by Rawls in the construction of his theory of justice because it seems quite clear to me (and to some others) that Rawls' philosophical procedures do not entail any specific primary moral principles such as 'human rights' that political considerations of social utility may, thence, recommend.[19] In Rawls' theory, then, coercion cannot be ruled out on the grounds of principle, for all citizens may 'originally' decide (i.e., by a presumed social contract) that coercion against the few may be unavoidably necessary for the increased social freedom of the many. In this case justice would be served, particularly since the democratic element of prior consent (to establish the authoritative use of coercion) was obtained. His conception of the social (pre-contractual) individual whose primary interests are best served by one kind of sociopolitical organization instead of by another incompatible one shows the normative character of both social freedom and coercion (in Rawls' theory).

In Marx's theory of society we also find a theory of human welfare, and this provides the elemental rationale for building the future ideal communist or 'classless' society, that is, one "in which the freedom of each is the condition for the free development of all." However, he depicts pre-communist, capitalist (and in some cases pre-capitalist or feudal) societies as driven by class struggles, by which is meant that one class perpetuates its domination over the other class(es) at the expense of the basic freedoms and need satisfactions of members of the downtrodden, immiserated laboring class(es). Marx presents us with a 'coercive model of society': it is borne of disharmony, dissensus, conflict, and alienation. He considers class warfare the essence of human existence in class societies. Sometimes the root antagonisms are submerged and subtle, and at other times they break out into open hostilities and violence.

The state is interpreted as 'organized coercion': it is a 'weapon' of class conflict. It is superimposed upon society because its task is to secure the interests of the economically dominant class while simultaneously it seeks to contain the basic conflicts and defuse possible revolutionary outbreaks. Support for revolutionary movements is encouraged by Marxists generally because it further contributes to what they consider to be historically inevitable, namely, socialist revolution. Modes of coexistence among opposing social classes, as portrayed in the Marxist literature, amount to accommodation and expedience and are, in the end, doomed to failure.

The demands of the coming communist society require a new sort of human individual to insure success: the bourgeois consciousness or the bourgeois' self-concept must be obliterated. What Marx means is, in part, modern society splits the individual in the following way: The human being has a divided consciousness—civil society and the state are separated from one another. The citizen of the state and the member of civil society are also separated. The person is presumably required to serve his or her own and others interests simultaneously.[20] The human individual is divided between the interests of his or her class and those of his or her citizenship, between private and public interests. The transformation of society's basic institutions (from economy to law, from education to politics) is necessary because individual human beings are not presumed by Marxists to be in essential or natural possession of basic human rights apart from organized society. Rather, it is only within the socialist state that a citizen acquires the basic rights and duties (owed him or her). Further, as implied in the new Soviet Constitution, only the individual citizen who is in possession of a socialist personality is entitled to the full status of the rights and duties accorded to citizens.[21] Marx's theory purports to be a descriptive (nonnormative) critique of modern society coupled with a normative set of proposals for and doctrines about the future ideal society, envisioned to have different social relations engaged in by qualitatively new ('socialist') types of persons.

In summary, the various theoretical and applied views, each involving coercion in some way, were selected from the areas of law, morality, and politics. Together they are seen to raise some interesting questions about how schemes of justification for normative (and nonnormative) conceptions of coercion are framed on the basis of an initial bias relating directly to underlying notions of personhood and to (priorities among) preferred values.

B. SOME PHILOSOPHICAL ISSUES RAISED BY DISPARATE INTERPRETATIONS AND APPLICATIONS OF THE TERM COERCION IN THE AREAS OF LAW, POLITICS, AND MORALITY

It is clear from the discussion in the last section that (1) in law and legal theory both normative and nonnormative conceptions of coercion can be found (e.g., involving freedom, consent, detriment, constraints); (2) in moral theory and ethics coercion is understood with regard to some presumed notion of prior individual freedom, autonomy, or rational agency but with normative and nonnormative variations, depending on the writer's final purpose; and (3) in politics and political theory the connection between some notion of coercion and the question of its justification are often merged as a means for evaluating the desirability or not of one type of system, ideology, or policy/ measure over some other competing types.

The boundary lines separating these areas in terms of their respective treatment of coercion are drawn merely for the purpose of analysis. In practice these boundary lines are usually blurred. For instance, legal definitions of coercion (in Anglo-American law) tend to embody pejorative preconceptions of (the elements of) coercion, so coercion is seen as *prima facie* illegal, as involving something unsuitable for ordinary citizens, as excuse-giving, or as a stronger form of responsibility—removal for actions (not) done. Hence, the legal definitions typically carry moral implications or stem from prior moral judgments associated with some held belief about the normative purpose of the institution of law as it applies to particular individuals in concrete, everyday situations involving matters of ethics and law.

The same may be said of political writings and everyday practices. Political societies are often broadly conceived in terms of various conflicting group interactions where the purpose is for each group to fulfill its basic interests, either alone or in concert with other groups. If each group is a 'circle of consent' (the cohesiveness of the group hinges on the common agreement among its members as to common purpose, etc.), interest fulfillment depends upon widening its 'circle of consent' or at least maintaining 'consent'. In any case, coercive domination of one group (or individual) by another bespeaks its inability to gain consent. The conceptual presuppostion of political analysis in this common view has its roots in both ethics and classical jurisprudence, the idea being that coercion is a form of injury: where consent is given, presumably no injury is done.

An important issue raised by the significance coercion received in these areas concerns the often unclarified treatment of coercion, namely, whether it is normative or nonnormative. The consequences in this regard for understanding coercion are serious because the elements of coercion may be ill defined (and so lend the term to tacit ideological interpretation) or may be presumed merely on the basis of an appeal to 'universal' values, ones everyone with good will or a standard of rationality is supposed to have.

Accordingly, the specific elements either included or recognized in the legal, political, and moral definitions of coercion must be explicitly stated. Judgments may then be made about whether the standard of (non)normativeness has been used tacitly or explicitly in framing a particular definition. The two-part issue that is important in this connection involves whether the sum of elements identified as constituting the definition of coercion is sufficient (1) to support a clear distinction between its normativeness or nonnormativeness, and (2) to avoid ideological bias in the conception of coercion.

If we have expected from any specific definition of coercion a precise statement of the (non)normative character of its basic elements, a brief review of the elements like 'freedom', 'consent', 'will', or 'constraints on actions', 'restrictions of freedom', and 'detrimental consequences' do not offer unequivocal assistance, for the review simply reminds us of the need to analyze the basic elements and not merely presuppose some preferred meaning of them. These notions (or 'elements') have received a wide variety of meanings, normative and nonnormative, as evidenced in the history of philosophical thought.

Some of many philosophical issues connected with how coercion is defined and which emerge in the areas of law, ethics, and political practice are as follows:

1. If coercion is conceived, as it often is, as a form of interference with someone's freedom, does consent by the 'coercee' to such interference, for better or worse, remove the coerciveness of the interference? Would this, then, not really count as 'interference' since the coercee consented to having his or her freedom restricted?

2. Is the victim's consent the only, or a more important, element in coercion as compared to 'freedom restriction'? If consent is defined as the exercise of freedom in making choices, is coercion limited to those instances in which the choices or options otherwise available to the 'victim' are restricted and restricted against his will? Is this what may be meant by constraints/restraints against performance?

3. Does the concept of coercion include instances where the 'victim's unwilling compliance' (a refusal to consent to) to do something is for his or her own good? Does coercion refer to freedom restrictions against one's will only in instances that result in the victim's detriment?

4. If coercion is defined as the violation of one's rights to freedom (i.e., one is entitled not to have his basic freedoms violated), does consent to

the rights violation—at the time of the violation—by the victim diminish its coerciveness? (One may consent to do something in violation of one's freedom right due perhaps to the greater disvalue attaching to the other possible alternatives, including not violating one's own such rights.)

NOTES

1. See Chapter 6 (p. 161) for an elaboration of my preferred definition of 'ideology'.

2. *The Plain Dealer*, Wednesday, March 23, 1983, p. 21a.

3. The Iowa Supreme Court seems to imply an affirmative response to the issues in (1) and a negative response to those in (2).

4. Coercion is being treated as a form of social control; a coercive *relationship* as involving more than two terms in its definition; and as having at least two essential, universally recognized elements: participants and actions of participants.

5. Coercion, as I interpret it, is a social concept. It is posited as being at least a three-term power relationship between at least two participants and an action. To review, the participants are the coercer and the coercee; the 'action' refers at least to some action the coercee performs.

6. The various possible modes of interrelatedness among participants depend upon how the participants are conceived. It permits a certain range of role possibilities perhaps excluded by different conceptions. For example, if one's self-identity as a person is socially formed and sustained, the conception of social relations and role possibilities will differ from a view assuming that self-identity stems from a pre-social or 'natural' human condition. In the latter case it is reasonable to suppose individual vs. individual or individual vs. society antagonisms, whereas the former allows no such opposition as far as basic interests are concerned.

7. Barbara Wootton, *Crime and the Criminal Law* (London: Stevens, 1963), to the "considerations of justice . . . [and of] prudence, may stand opposed to a particular prescription of strict penal liability" view (noted by Hyman Gross, *A Theory of Criminal Justice,* New York: Oxford University Press, 1979).

8. In case law we find coercion defined as "compulsion," "constraint," "compelling by force of arms or threat." *General Motors v. Blevins,* D.C. Colo., 144 F. Supp. 381, 384. Also, coercion has been used to define 'duress': any conduct that overpowers will and coerces and constrains performance of an act which otherwise would not have been performed. *Williams v. Rentz Banking Co.,* 112 Ga. App. 384, 145 S.E. 256, 258.

9. *Black's Law Dictionary,* 5th ed. (St. Paul, Minn.: West, 1979), p. 234.

10. Louis Henkin, "Privacy and Autonomy," *Columbia Law Review* 74 (December 1974), pp. 1410-11.

11. Stuart Hampshire, ed. *Public and Private Morality* (Cambridge: Cambridge University Press, 1979, p. 20.

12. H. J. Paton, tr., *Kant: The Moral Law* (London: Hutchinson, 1956), pp. 19, 108-9.

13. See Carl Friedrich's *The Philosophy of Law in Historical Perspective* (Chicago: University of Chicago Press, 1963), p. 127.

14. See, for example, Michael Taylor's vision of the noncoercive society in his work: *Community, Anarchy, and Liberty* (New York: Cambridge University Press, 1982).

15. Ralf Dahrendorf, *Class and Class Conflict in Industrial Society* (Stanford Calif.: Stanford University, 1959), p. 162.

16. John Somerville, *The Philosophy of Marxism* (Minneapolis: MEP Publications, 1983), p. 100. Someone sympathetic to Marxism might argue that "force and violence are not *necessary* parts of the Marxist concept of revolution" (p. 122).

17. See works that deal with this question: Hannah Arendt, *Between Past and Future* (New York: Viking Press, 1968), p. 17; Sheldon Wolin, "Political Theory as a Vocation," *American Political Science Review* 63 (December 1969); and John Gunnell, *Philosophy, Science and Political Inquiry* (Morristown, N.J.: General Learning Press, 1975), pp. 246-63.

18. *The Republic*, in *Dialogues of Plato* (New York: Random House, 1937), vol. I. B. Jowett, tr. pp. 698, 706; see also R. S. Brumbaugh, *The Philosophers of Greece* (Albany: State University of New York Press, 1981), p. 168.

19. See John Rawls, *A Theory of Justice* (Cambridge, Mass.: The Belknap Press of Harvard University, 1971); see also John Gray, "J.S. Mill on Liberty, Utility and Human Rights," in *Human Rights: NOMOS XXIII*, J. R. Pennock and J. W. Chapman, eds. (New York: New York University Press, 1981), p. 108.

20. From Marx's "The Communist Manifesto," in *Karl Marx: Selected Writings*, David McClellan, ed. (New York: Oxford University Press, 1977), p. 238; see also Robert C. Tucker, "Marx as a Political Theorist," in Marx's *Socialism*, Shlomo Avineri, ed. (New York: Lieber-Atherton, 1973), pp. 130-35; and Marx's "On the Jewish Question," in McClellan, p. 46.

21. For example, see Article 14: "The source of the growth of social wealth and of the well-being of the people, and of each individual, is the labor, free from exploitation, of Soviet people. The state exercises control over the measure of labor and of consumption in accordance with the principle of socialism: 'From each according to his ability, to each according to his work.' Socially useful work and its results determine a

person's status in society . . . the state helps transform labor into the prime vital needs of every Soviet citizen.'' Again in Article 39: ''Enjoyment by citizens of their rights and freedoms must not be to the detriment of the interests of society or the state, or infringe the rights of other citizens.'' From the text of the Constitution (Fundamental Law) of the Union of Soviet Socialist Republics, adopted October 7, 1977, in *Great Soviet Encyclopedia,* vol. 31, trans. of 3rd ed., (New York: Macmillan, 1982).

CHAPTER 2

The Conceptual Framework of Coercion

The goal of this chapter is to introduce a preliminary conceptual or analytical framework towards a working definition of *coercion*. The analysis will proceed in the next several chapters to formulate an operational definition of *coercion*. The definition will be framed in nonnormative terms of scientific discourse but with the aim that it be sufficiently dynamic to be applied in normative discussions of coercion without dissolving altogether the traditional conceptual distinction between empirical (social) facts and (normative) social values.

The recent philosophical literature on coercion could be categorized as having one of two different approaches: the normative and the nonnormative (examples of each type of theory will be cited later in this chapter). Both approaches have had ideological associations. Many so-called nonnormative approaches have been implicitly ideological while normative approaches have sometimes been explicitly ideological or too closely aligned with the patterns of thought of a particular ideology to be considered independently. Other theories both normative and nonnormative are not sufficiently powerful to account for coercion in its variegated social context. This present treatment of coercion will aim at an analysis of coercion in its social context; considerations in this regard will eventually bring in issues that bear on normative values. However, we need to establish a working terminology as a first step towards a theory that will take into account the dynamic and social essence of coercion and simultaneously avoid an uncritical ideological bias.

This chapter should not be considered separately from the one(s) that follows because, by itself, it does not reflect what I believe to be the dynamic, multidimensional aspects of coercion as a social phenomenon. Although we cannot, in the final analysis, account for coercion as independent of its social context, we must for present purposes lift it out of context to examine it. As we will be using common language terminology that introduces some confusions, it is important to clarify the range of meaning of each term of analysis as it is used in this volume. Ultimately the analysis will show that the term 'coercion' refers to a class of 'social events' of a given type—a type of social relationship and, as such, an abstraction.

Among instances of coercion and of similar events or relationships, boundaries are formed that may sometimes seem clearly drawn to distinguish coercion from other types of event/relationships. However, in other cases the vagueness of the boundaries seems more evident and causes one type of event/relationship to shade off subtly into others. This is not unique to coercion but is characteristic of a dynamic view of social phenomena in general.

The present chapter will focus on the major functional unit in the theory: the *elemental categories* of coercion. I will define the meaning of *elemental category* and other important terminology and will then specify what fulfills these categories and their associated roles with respect to an 'act' of coercion.

PROCEDURES

Identification of a Classification System

We shall begin by focussing on the type and structure of the classification system being used as an analytical framework for the larger social theory. In a sense, this structure can be regarded as a blueprint for the definition of coercion that follows in later chapters. Both the definition of coercion and the component units of analysis are framed in ordinary language terms. These terms may have been used in other theories in similar ways and also colloquially as common abstractions. Nevertheless, they are used in this study as clear, consistent, and practical (i.e., operational) terms that will now be defined.

The word *term* refers to the separate units of thought or ideas expressed in a definition of coercion but conveys no distinction between such ideas as to their objectifiability. Thus, any definition or theory behind the meaning of coercion concerns a certain number of terms, only some of which are constant, objectifiable features we shall call an 'elemental category'.

The *elemental category* (hereafter abbreviated EC) is the major fundamental unit of analysis for a social theory or a definition of human interaction such as the one envisioned here. Such a theory may be said to possess a certain totality of ECs on its most abstract plane of analysis. As we shall demonstrate, some social theories differ from others depending upon, for example, the nature and number (and perhaps, meaning) of the essential ECs that constitute them. Because an EC has a limited range of suitable values assigned to it by a given definition of human interaction, it functions as a logical constant with respect to that theory as a whole.

A logical constant has been called a 'relational variable' because, unlike other variables that are symbols with no specified meaning, the scope of its meaning has been restricted by definition or theory, as when a member of a class stands in that relation to the class of which it is a member. I will use the expression 'constant feature'. But, in any case, this is to be distinguished from a real or physical constant of human experience such as the speed of light, with a fixed numerical value assigned to its symbolic abbreviation as used in science, c.

In the present theory, an EC will also be understood to function as a dynamic entity with respect to that theory. The EC is not a minimal unit but is to be understood as a larger class, representing a constellation of (at least) all the necessary and sufficient objectifiable 'elements in the set or range of values of a given elemental category' (EC^x). In any given social theory where elements e^1, e^2 . . . e^n are consistent with each other and with the theory's basic requirements, we may then state that $(e^1, e^2 . . . e^n) \equiv EC^x$. (The sign for logical equivalence is " $\equiv$ "; "." is the sign for logical conjunction of discrete propositions.)

Later in this chapter we shall use the concept of an elemental category (EC) to analyze and identify the primary objectifiable constituents of a given definition of coercion. In fact, several different definitions that are found in the literature will be selected to show how this classification scheme, which we have begun to describe, works. As we shall observe, a definition may contain any number of essential terms or ideas, some of which are not easily classifiable as ECs, perhaps because they are nonobjectifiable or at least not objectifiable in the same sense as the ECs are. But like the ECs, the other features or terms of a definition (the non-ECs) may be either 'constant' or 'variable' aspects of the definition. Therefore, a good analysis of coercion must be based on a classification scheme that can show such distinctions between the various terms of a definition without distorting the nature of their importance in the definition and of their (or, more precisely, their referents') being.

A *feature,* f, is a descriptive attribute and a minimal unit with respect to the larger functional classes or ECs in the social theory. (As we will suggest, an element is a type of a feature.) However, any given feature qualifies as a possible descriptive unit that is sometimes but not always necessary. Therefore, as I mean the term, a feature may be a constant, f^c, or a variable, f^v, with respect to the whole theory or more properly with respect to the classes on the next highest level of abstraction, the EC. A constant feature (a 'relational' or 'constant' variable is intended to mean the same as constant feature, though the former are the more usual expressions found in the philosophic literature) is also an element (f^c = e).

An *element*, e, refers to a minimal essential unit in an analysis of a social theory. It is a specific descriptive attribute or feature of an EC and typically (but not invariably) functions as a 'constant feature' (or 'logical constant') of an EC in a given social theory. By 'constant feature' is meant a symbolic generalization (e) of what it is supposed to represent by being assigned a limited value or range of values by the theory or a definition. (In contrast, some variables are unrestricted generalizations and receive upon interpretation any specified values or range of values.) Elements are the basic or essential components of a given theory's EC, however, an EC may also be composed of additional ingredients besides 'elements'. These additional, nonelemental features of a theory are variable though specific to a given theory (but perhaps not to others); they contribute to the overall elaboration of it, though by definition they are not necessary constituents of the theory.

An *instance,* I, of an EC is a specific combination of elements and variables that together could constitute a given fulfillment of an elemental category.

An *event/relationship*, e/r, is the sum of all instances or the fulfillment of all the elemental categories and other features that, in the given social theory, would be sufficient to cause the 'coercion' event to occur. An e/r is neither simply an 'action' nor a 'relationship', as these chapters will show.

Finally, we recognize a *role* component, R, of an EC. Much human interaction occurs in the context of the various social roles assumed by the participants. We should be clear at this point about what is meant here by 'role' because the conception of coercion being proposed will eventually be seen to be based in large measure on the notion of 'social role'. Accordingly, we shall use the term 'role' in this study in two different ways or with two separate meanings. 'Role' refers to how each of the most abstract categories of elements functions with respect to the larger social theory but also with regard to the ECs recognized in either the theory or a definition of coercion. Thus, for instance, if we suppose that 'human beings' and 'human actions' represent different basic elements of categorization in a given theory (definition), one not being simply reducible to the other, both play similar abstract classificatory roles in the theory (as ECs), though the latter may be a logico-practical extension of the former and so stands in a certain position or role in relation to the other.

The other meaning of role is the sense of 'role' as a basic unit of *social* analysis. It refers to the different types and basis for human relationships. This sense of the term is most important for my analysis of coercion and so will be examined at the appropriate time. However, at this time, to better grasp the meaning of an EC, it is necessary to define formally what its basic constituents are.

Let us consider a hypothetical construct of these terms. Let

A. EC^x

$$f^1 \quad f^2 \quad f^3 \quad f^4 \quad f^5$$

A. Elemental category (x) is a hypothetical class made up of five features all of which are constants and so are essential to the specific characterization of EC^x.

$$f^1 \ldots \ldots f^5 = f^c$$

f = feature
f^c = constant feature (or e)
e = element (or f^c)
f^v = variable feature
EC = Elemental Category
e/r = event/relationship
I = instance of EC
R = role ('social role')

B. This hypothetical class of EC^y is made up of $f^1 \ldots f^5$, which are constants and are essential to EC^y (and are not mutually exclusive). $f^{16} \ldots f^{18}$ are variable features of EC^y, and each is possible but not all are possible (i.e., mutually inclusive) because some are mutually exclusive.

B.

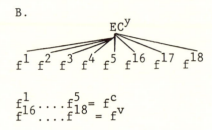

EC^x and EC^y are each theoretical constructs of an EC (elemental category). EC^x could meet the minimum specifications for an instance, I, but EC^y could not because EC^y includes mutually exclusive or inconsistent features among its f^v.

C.

C. EC^z is another hypothetical construct of EC that could be an instance because the variable features are shown as subtypes of the constant features (or elements) that are themselves mutually exclusive.

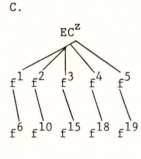

The two hypothetical examples, EC^x and EC^z, could meet the specifications to be an instance, I, of an EC in an event/relationship, e/r, but we must realize that *any particular* instance of EC may be constructed differently. Actually EC^x and EC^z may be structured symbolic formats of the same instance, but EC^z provides more details by giving more information about the constant features ($f^1 \ldots f^5$).

An EC may also be structured like EC^y *if* $f^{16} \ldots f^{18}$ are specified as being variable features that are not mutually exclusive.

For our present purpose, it is important to stress that an EC is a functional unit in our theory and that the role(s) of certain pertinent ECs bears certain critical connections to other roles of an EC. The *structure* of any given EC in the theory may be different from that of all other ECs in the theory provided that it is logically consistent with the component elements of each particular EC.

ECs AND COERCION

Now that we have illustrated the basic structure of a social theory of this type, we will start to show how it works with respect to coercion. (In the ensuing chapters we will specify the nature of the features of the various elemental categories.) In this section we will merely identify and define in a preliminary way the ECs that constitute *coercion*. There are four ECs in the suggested social theory of coercion: coercer, instrument, coercee, and behavior. The proposed definitions below will be refined further in the coming chapters.

The *coercer,* P, is one of at least two necessary participants in any coercive event, the other being the coercee, Q, whom we will discuss below. Inasmuch as coercion is conceived here as a social relationship of a certain kind among human beings, its participants never include nonhuman life-forms and agents of causation (as we noted in Chapter 1). We have also assumed that social coercion is an act and form of power. Consequently, in the power relationship existing between the participants in the coercive event, it is the coercer to whom the balance of power belongs (and in cases of coercion, the possession of power is a matter of degree; it is incorrect to presume that the coercee or victim is absolutely powerless in relation to the coercer). Accordingly, there is a transitive power relationship between the coercer and the coercee in terms of which the causal link between their respective behaviors is framed.

Although no coercive event is conceivable without a 'coercer', despite that some definitions exclude any reference to it, some writers refer to all the participants as 'actors', and 'agents', as well as 'sources' and 'victims'. This usage is not objectionable once we are clear about what we mean by 'actor' (or by that particular) and so on. The dominant tendency in scientific analyses of coercion is to interpret 'actor' in terms of a certain preconception of what it means to be a human being. In itself this is not objectionable. The present analysis will seek to avoid subtle ideological attributions in its characterization of the coercer (and coercee), which occurs too often in the writings of social scientists, and will acknowledge implicit ideological and political affinities when appropriate.

The preferred conception of the human being underlying the 'coercer' (and coercee) is as follows. The coercer is (1) a rational being in the sense of being able to formulate 'reasons' and act on them in terms of a conscious life-plan; (2) a being whose sphere of autonomy is defined in relation to other similar beings, and, in the context of coercion, in relation to the other(s) who is involved with one in a specific power relation; and (3) a being whose freedom and will to achieve his or her life-plan depend mainly upon the proper consideration of the relevant desires, interests, needs, and rights. This is only a partial characterization, but for now it suffices to allow a better description of the elemental category of coercer/participant.

In any given instance of coercion, the coercer can be conceived as being an individual human being or a collectivity of individuals; or it can be a coercing agency, by which is meant someone who is acting in an instrumentalized fashion: for example, a police officer, judge, or manager who attempts through his or her behavior (at least in theory) to carry into effect the rules, policies, and directives of the respective establishments for which they work. The coercer, P, is a human actor (individual, group, or agent) who is socially autonomous with respect to the human victim/coercee, Q, and whose behavior, p, controls the behavior, q, of Q in a certain way. In this sense then, P is a coercer only with respect to the specific type of power relationship P has with Q (namely, one where Q's behavior, q, is being coercively controlled by P's doing p).

The *instrument*, p, is an action or agent of P that is sufficient to cause a certain coerced behavior, q, of Q. The instrument of coercion is the means by which the action done under coercion is effectuated. A coerced action can be the result of any of a number of possible instruments. Those most commonly associated with coercion are physical force and threats to use force. It is noted here but will be examined in detail later that coercion and physical force are not the same thing as many are inclined to suppose. Instead, physical force is an instrument, among others, of coercion and not its essence; for coercion can be shown to occur in the absence of physical force. Other techniques for influencing someone's behavior, such as paternalism, manipulation, psychosurgery, bribes, incentives, and offers, will be of considerable interest when we attempt in the coming chapters to further distinguish coercion from its various instruments, as well as to demarcate the often blurry boundary line between the coercive and noncoercive aspects of these techniques.

What makes an action of P coercive—an instrument and a necessary feature in the analysis of coercion—is the type of effect or influence it has on Q with respect to Q's behavior. Thus, 'instruments' are coercive only in the context of an interaction and relation between P and Q. An agent of P acquires coerciveness in the same way, but the term 'agent' refers here to the techniques and tools (that may or may not include actions) that P uses to coerce Q: a gun becomes an instrument of coercion not by itself but as it is wielded or as it functions in P's relationship with Q. Similarly, a soldier can become an instrument or agent of coercion depending upon the orders received from his or her superior. Thus, an instrument of coercion may be the coercer's action or something the coercer uses to control the victim's behavior in the manner desired.

The *coercee,* Q, refers to the person or persons being coerced by P and for that reason has often been called the 'victim'. The elemental role of coercee is the opposite side of the power-based social relationship between participants, P and Q. We must first establish the nature of any conceived coercee before we can offer an adequate description of what fulfills the elemental role of coercee, which is really the final aim of this entire analysis: what it is that allows us to claim Q has been coerced. Here we concentrate only on Q.

The features of the participant whom we call 'coercee' are no different from those enumerated under coercer above (1), (2), and (3). The difference lies in where Q stands in relation to P in their transitive power relationship. That is, the coercee, Q, loses some autonomy with respect to the coercer, P, in the sense that his behavior, q, is controlled in some manner by P's behavior, p. Q is the being whose preexistent autonomy is negated in some fashion by P and whose power over certain of his own actions has been usurped by P. However, this does not mean that Q is powerless to control any of his or her own behavior. For if he or she was, no autonomy of Q's as a social being could be compromised by anything P does, and so a coercive relation between P and Q would be inconceivable.

The coercive event/relationship, e/r, always involves, as we noted, at least two participants, coercer and coercee. This is a *relational* view of coercion. Thus, for someone to have been coerced, some other party is presumed to have done the coercing.

The *behavior*, q, of the coercee, Q, is what Q does as a causal result of P's doing (or not doing) p; it is the action Q takes under coercion. Coerced behavior is, nonetheless, a type of human behavior in general, and this consideration is equally applicable to coercer and coercee alike. It is distinguishable from the forms of behavior that are not 'action' movements (sneezing, slipping, and so on). In short, q and p are 'action' behaviors of Q and P respectively when and only when the former are causally linked to the choices of the latter to perform them. Hence, control among Q's motives for doing (or not doing) q is the direct result of something P did or did not do with respect to Q. Thus, the behavior of the participants in a coercive e/r (event/relationship) is conceptualized on the basis of the key notion of choice. 'Having a choice' means that at least one alternative course of action is available to the participant at the moment the behavior is expressed (e.g., choosing not to do something still counts as an action).

In the course of analyzing coercion it will be necessary to refine this distinction about choice-based behavior as it applies to the coercee's behavior, q, (i.e., the action done under coercion) to enable us to distinguish between physical (and other kinds of) coercion and (uncoerced) physical movements such as being pushed unexpectedly off a bicycle by someone else, or movements that result from being panic-stricken and, perhaps, to distinguish between 'having a choice' and 'having someone else predetermine the available choices'.

Being a constant feature or elemental category, EC, in our analysis of coercion, q cannot be understood ultimately as causally independent of P, p, and Q's relation to them. Thus, to assert the proposition 'P coerces Q to do q' we must mean that in part, q is in some sense the direct consequence of the coercer's use of some instrument, p, which coerces.

ELEMENTAL CATEGORIES IN SOME
CURRENT DEFINITIONS OF COERCION

There are other treatments of coercion that have categorized these ECs differently. (Actually, the terms used by others are not really called 'elemental category'; however, an EC would be analogous in its function as a major operational unit.) My theory has four major units (ECs); some other writers have supposed a different number, often two or three terms.

To understand better the significance of this conception, we shall present a brief review of some contemporary literature on coercion and its related concepts. As we shall notice, some definitions contain certain features that are not commonly regarded as objectifiable but that nonetheless are crucial to the definition. Our analysis will attempt not to obscure their status but to acknowledge the existence of such subjective (or intersubjective) features and to describe their relative place with respect to the elemental category in the given definition.

We look at a definition (of coercion) to grasp the author's concept because it is from this that one can discern what is considered to be the minimally necessary features to describe a certain phenomenon.

In our composite of his comments about what coercion is, J. R. Pennock seems to mean "someone's exercising power by using force."[1] In this implied definition the focus is placed squarely upon the main participant or coercer and upon his 'coercive activity of forcing or using force', presumably as an instrument in the act of coercion. Pennock also explicitly introduces the concept of power into the definition but as an exercising of someone's 'power' rather than as a 'power relationship'.

On the face of it, there are two concepts expressed here that conform to our proposed elemental categories: namely, 'someone's exercising power' (analogous to the coercer, P) and force, which might be categorized as an instrument of coercion, p, in our schema. Pennock apparently believes that "force," although objectifiable in his view, is an entity that can be 'used' by P and thus is *an action of* P. A less limiting definition might include other 'instruments' besides force that could be used to coerce. Indeed, it appears to be erroneous to confuse 'coercion' with only one of its instruments inasmuch as coercion may be a consequence from other instrumental actions of P, such as threats, bribes, or other inducements. While certain instances of these other instrumental actions may be classified as an indirect or mediated use of force, other instances clearly cannot, and thus it seems to me that to equate 'force' with all instrumental actions of P is an undue inflation of the meaning of the term force.

Conspicuously absent from Pennock's definition is any reference to the victim of coercion—the coercee, Q, in our schema—or for that matter any behavior of Q (viz., q) that would indicate that a 'successful' act of coercion has occurred. Pennock does refer to these other aspects in his analysis, but he clearly does not consider them as essential to his proposed definition. Such considerations are ostensibly accounted for by the inclusion of the term 'power' as an essential feature. That Pennock has chosen to include the term 'power' may itself be the most significant aspect of his definition.

As future chapters of this volume will address, the concept of power comes to the very heart of the role relationship(s) characteristic of any act of coercion. Nevertheless, Pennock does not actually acknowledge the existence of such relationships. Not only has he deemphasized the importance of including the coercee as participant, but even his analysis of power lacks certain key references to related subjective and intersubjective phenomena that can be shown to characterize the role relationship in the coercive event/relationship, e/r.

By some accounts Pennock has offered a three-term definition of coercion in his inclusion of three elemental features: the coercer ('someone'), 'force', and 'power'; yet in another sense, his view can be regarded as only a *two-category* definition. 'Power', although appropriately included as a constant feature, should not be considered as an elemental category in that it is not objectifiable in the same way as either the participant(s) or the participant's behavior is objectifiable. While Pennock's usage of "power" as a term may suggest the existence of a role relationship (between the coercer and, by implication, his victim) it does not explicitly account for roles either in the definition or the ensuing analysis (from which we distill his view from his 'overview' of others' positions). Thus Pennock's view may be classified as a nonrelational, two-category definition. It is nonrelational because it lacks any specific reference to a determinate relationship between at least two participants in a power, if not a coercive, social e/r.

H. J. McCloskey also uses a coercer-centered approach in defining coercion; however, his two-category definition is more elaborate than Pennock's because it includes four or five terms. McCloskey defines coercion as "power exercised by a determinate person(s), organization(s) . . . by the use of threats backed by sanctions in terms of evils to be imposed, benefits to be withdrawn or not conferred."[2] The terms are 'power', the coercer ['person(s)', 'organization(s)'], and 'evils to be imposed, benefits to be withdrawn or not conferred.' We would have only four terms if we classify the sorts of sanctions mentioned under "backed by sanctions"; otherwise, there are five terms. Again, coercion is defined as what someone (person, organization) does in using certain kinds of threats. It is a nonrelational definition, though the author implies the existence of a victim. Accordingly, we identify the coercer, P, and the instrument of coercion, p (threats), as the two elemental categories.

The rationale behind our exclusion of terms other than P and p in McCloskey's definition as being ECs stems from two important considerations, each corresponding to a different term, namely, 'power' and 'backed by sanctions'. In the instance of McCloskey's usage concerning 'power', again, as in Pennock's case, the absence of an explicit role relationship embodied in the definition in terms of which a power relationship (and not simply an exercise of someone's power) may be specified, means that there is little by which 'power' can, in his definition, be objectified, despite that all instances involve 'power' considerations. With respect to the other important expression (term), 'backed by sanctions', the role played by a personal value system or by subjective values becomes amplified in attempts at defining what makes coercion successful. To threaten to visit some 'evil' upon someone who does not share with the threatener the same estimate of what was evidently intended as a serious threat, thus rendering the threat-making

utterance or gesture nugatory, suggests the importance of incor-
porating into one's definition of coercion the relevant considerations involving objective matters. Therefore such subjective
matters should not receive, in our efforts to classify the definitions
which contain them, equal footing, as it were, with the elemental
categories. Yet they may be treated as constant features of
coercion.

A three-term but two-category definition in line with the broader
problem we have been alluding to, namely, scientific attempts to
comprehend social phenomena, is Harry Frankfurt's. For Frankfurt,
coercion invariably involves an "imposition of one's will on
another."[3] In his view, the essence of coercion lies in the effect
someone has on another and not on the instrument used to bring
about the coercive effect. 'Threats', 'offers', and 'physical force'
are all considered possible instruments, or in his terminology,
means of coercion, but he does not include these in any way as
explicit components of his definition. His is a coercee-centered
definition, even though definite reference is made to a coercer. The
three terms are the *coercer,* the imposition of the *coercer's will*, and
the other (presumably, the coercee). Frankfurt's definition leaves
unstated (but it implies) that it is the 'will' of the coercee that is
being imposed upon, in which case, there are really four terms: the
two participants and the 'will' of each. Insofar as it recognizes a
certain relation between participants—between the will of the
coercer and another—the definition is relational.[4] Yet, the only two
objectifiable features contained in this definition are the two
participants. Hence, it is a two-category definition.

In contrast, we find a variation on this definition given by
Bernard Dauenhauer where there are three elemental categories
instead of the two found in Frankfurt's definition. Dauenhauer's
definition reads: coercion is "the use of techniques and physical
implements to impose one's will on another."[5] Accordingly, the
instrument, p, of coercion is acknowledged in this definition along
with the two participants whose coercive relationship is specified in
terms of P's 'imposition of his will' on Q. The relationship between
P and Q is mediated by their respective 'wills'. In this case the
number of ECs also corresponds to the number of terms expressed
in the definition.

A different reading of the same definition is where only the instruments used for coercion are objectifiable since a 'will' is not; nor are two 'wills' standing in some putative relationship to each other. In order to discern just how many ECs this definition contains, it is necessary first to recognize that the term 'will' (as in 'one's will') is not objectifiable in the same sense as the being whose 'will' it is. But since the definition does explicitly mention two participants, to each of whom belongs a 'will' believed to be inseparable from his or her identity, we may assess this as a three-category definition.

Apart from the question of the conception of the subjectivity (or nonobjectivity) of the human will found in both Frankfurt's and Dauenhauer's definitions, a related question is raised in connection with the presumption that seems to be behind their definitions. It concerns the notion of the will's 'inviolability': not that someone's will cannot be violated but that it is always wrong to do so. This normative implication, however important it may be, is not as crucial for our present purpose as the observation that neither of these definitions seems to express an awareness on the part of their authors of the subjectivity involved in the presumption of an 'inviolable' individual will and not only of a 'will'. I do not suggest that definitions of coercion must be stated in completely objectifiable terms but rather that definitions that contain subjective terms should not be treated as if they were wholly 'objective'. Thus, the schema being proposed and applied in this chapter has been designed to illuminate this distinction by classifying the various terms in accordance with how they function in the given definition.

Our use of the distinction between a 'term' of a definition and an 'elemental category' of a definition is seen to be especially valuable with respect to the next definition to be introduced, for its author claims that his own definition of coercion is an advance over a certain other definition because his contains three terms whereas the other has only two, thereby making his own a relational definition. This claim has merit for that reason alone, but his 'term' analysis fails to assess the significance of the 'subjective' features in relation to the 'objective' ones. As a result, classification of the coerciveness of certain events or relationships becomes more arbitrary since it depends on the number of identifiable terms present in a given case and not on the type of terms and the conceptual relation between them.

Coercion, states Martin Gunderson, is someone's "use of or threat of the use of force against the permission of the victim and concerns the use, type, degree, and occasion of force used."[6] Again the notion of force occupies a central position in a definition of coercion. In any case, we can distinguish at least four terms, perhaps more if we are to isolate as separate variables or terms the 'occasion' and 'degree' of force used. In other words, we have identified the (1) coercer ('someone'), (2) the instrument ('use of or threat of the use of force'), (3) 'against the permission', and (4) the coercee (or 'victim').

Gunderson's analysis of coercion and of the primary place of force in its definition is certainly more subtle than Pennock's and perhaps more developed than Michael Bayles'[7] whose treatment his own stems from, but we find some degree of arbitrariness in the way he has identified only three terms in his definition. He considers the only terms to be the coercer, the coercee, and the action done under coercion.

If we inspect his definition closely, we discover no mention of the 'action done under coercion'. Certainly the 'coerced action' is implicit in the statement that force is being used against the victim's permission, for what is evidently meant by Gunderson is that the victim is coerced in being made to do something against his permission: this is what the 'victimization' of the coercee consists of, not merely that the other is 'witholding permission'.

The three terms I recognize (the two participants and the instrument) are, by contrast, explicitly evidenced in the definition. For some unknown reason, Gunderson has ignored the distinction between the coercer and the instrument of coercion (including both what implement is used to coerce as well as the action of the coercer that also may coerce as in 'physical' coercion), and these are two clearly objectifiable and distinguishable, constant features that must be acknowledged in any accurate analysis of his definition. However, Gunderson's mention of two types of instruments, force and threats, indicates that each is a variable feature, f^v, of his definition because some e/r's may result from the use of one rather than the other instrument.

We should notice the presence of an additional ingredient in Gunderson's definition that contributes to its overall set of descriptive features, but while it is certainly a 'term' of the definition, it does not function as an elemental catgegory. It is the victim's 'lack of permission' in performing the action he is supposed to do under coercion. Though this term may be a constant feature of a definition of coercion, and hence common to all instances of coercion, is it to be classified as objectifiable in the same or similar sense that the victim's coerced behavior is, though it certainly is assumed by Gunderson to be something done (or not done, as the case may be) by the coercee?

Parallel expressions such as 'withholding consent', 'against the will,' or 'denial of choice' raise the same question as 'failure to give permission', namely, how is 'permission' to be understood in our analysis of coercion and, in particular, of Gunderson's view? Does it describe a subjective phenomenon, despite the fact that its most common modes of bodily expression give the observer an objective basis for inferring its presence (e.g., a nod of the head, utterance, or suitable gesture, and so on)? In short, I argue that 'consent', 'permission', and 'willingness' are not phenomena ultimately reducible to external objective body movements.

Nevertheless, such terms are commonly found in definitions such as Gunderson's. It should also be observed that some definitions of coercion contain no word or reference to these terms; moreover, in some cases (such as the one Gunderson develops, viz., Bayles') coercion is defined on the basis of the presence (and not the absence or negation) of consent (or choice). For instance, Bayles makes the claim that in some cases of coercion, the coercee *deliberately* performs the action he is coerced into doing (he calls this 'dispositional' as opposed to 'physical' coercion). Evidently he has in mind that the coercee in such cases invariably has some *choice*: yield to the coercer's demand or suffer the threatened or implied sanction for refusal. In being coerced, then, the coercee is held deliberately to do, or to do by choice, what he does under coercion. Although writers may differ about the role of consent in a definition of coercion, our chief concern at this point is to distinguish the presence of this type of term from the objectifiable terms in a definition. In due course we shall examine the relevancy of the domain of intersubjectivity as it contributes to an

understanding of the phenomenon of coercion in one important
respect by stressing the value of not objectifying 'subjective' terms.

The last definition selected for mention in this section belongs to
Cheyney Ryan, who clearly states that coercion as a normative
concept is a relation between at least two participants where the
action(s) of one, P, infringes on the personal liberty of the other
participant, Q, and where P prevents Q from (1) exercising an
important right, q^1, or (2) discharging an important duty, q^2, with
respect to someone's basic right.[8] In this definition there are at least
five terms: the two participants (P, Q); the instrumental action (p)
and the action (q^1, q^2) of Q; and the infringed-upon liberty of Q.
The objectifiable actions and participants qualify this as a four-
category definition. What remains problematical is how to classify
the 'personal liberty' (of Q) inasmuch as no definitive conclusion
has been reached within the history of philosophy as to whether
'personal freedom' is an 'objective' concept; indeed, there are
myriad senses, both purportedly objective and subjective, of the
term.

In Ryan's definition we find 'personal liberty' qualified by a
putative 'right to exercise one's liberty in some specific way'.
Therefore, such 'freedom', r, seems to mean a condition for Q's
doing or not doing something protected by some entitlement; it is
not a feature of Q's action. The exercise of actions covered by some
such entitlement is a constant feature, f^c, of Ryan's definition,
regardless of whether it refers to Q's duty, corresponding to
someone else's right or to Q's right claimed 'against the world at
large'. On the other hand, duty-based or right-based actions are
variable features ($f^v = f^r \cdot f^d$) of the definition.

In the next chapter we will offer a more thorough discussion of
the place of subjectivity and intersubjectivity in a scientific world
view and more particularly in definitions of coercion. This
discussion will be very important to an elaboration of this writer's
own view of coercion. Also, because so many definitions include
terms the subjective qualities of which tend to obstruct efforts at
eliminating arbitrariness and ambiguity from definitions, it is
essential to be clear about identification of the objectifiable as well
as the nonobjectifiable terms of a definition. Such terms as human
'will', 'choice', 'motive', 'consent', 'intention', 'reason', 'moral
sense', and even 'responsibility' and 'freedom' figure as promi-

nently in most definitions of coercion as do participants (P, Q), their instruments (p), and behavior (p, q). For example, the notion of 'will' is found in a definition such as 'P compels Q to unwillingly do q'. It is our aim both to examine the significance of the subjective features of a definition and to specify their conceptual relation to the objectifiable features of it.

NOTES

1. J. R. Pennock, "Coercion: An Overview," in *Coercion: NOMOS XIV*, J. R. Pennock and J. W. Chapman, eds. (Chicago: Aldine-Atherton Press, 1972), pp. 6, 7.

2. H. J. McCloskey, "Coercion: Its' Nature and Significance," *Southern Journal of Philosophy* (Fall 1980), p. 340.

3. Harry Frankfurt, "Coercion and Moral Responsibility," in *Essays on Freedom of Action,* Ted Honderich, ed. (London: Routledge & Kegan Paul, 1973), p. 83.

4. The putative relationship between two wills is analogous to what in the Law of Contracts is called a "meeting of the minds" as a condition of contract formation. However, in law, this has become nothing more than a 'figure of speech', a relic no longer used because of its elusive subjectivity; in philosophy, on the other hand, its elusiveness, has never been a bar to use.

5. Bernard Dauenhauer, "Politics and Coercion," *Philosophy Today* (July 1978), p. 109.

6. Martin Gunderson, "Threats and Coercion," *Canadian Journal of Philosophy* 9, 2 (June 1979), p. 248.

7. Michael Bayles, "A Concept of Coercion," in *Coercion,* Pennock and Chapman, eds., pp. 16-29.

8. Cheyney Ryan, "The Normative Concept of Coercion," *Mind* 89 (October 1980), p. 491.

CHAPTER 3

Role, Intersubjectivity, and Coercion

Up to this point in our analysis, we have approached 'coercion' from a deliberately one-dimensional perspective, outlining the elemental categories from an empirical point of departure. Thus, we have identified the following objective criteria as essential features in a definition of coercion:

1) Coercer (P) → 2) instrument of coercion (p)
3) Coercee (Q) → 4) coerced behavior (q)

Whereas the above categories may have observable and/or quantifiable correlates for each possible act of coercion, they are not in themselves wholly sufficient to specify both the dynamic and relational character of the concept. We may regard the elemental categories as forming an empirical cornerstone for our present treatment of coercion, but we should be mindful of their inherent limitations.

There is certainly precedent in the philosophical literature for recognizing that coercion may extend beyond empirical boundaries. In this chapter we shall recall definitions of coercion in which appear such nonobjective terms as *permission, will, choice, wish, intent*, among others, but which tend to treat such notions on the same footing as the empirical categories of 'participant' and 'action'. While the concepts to which such nonobjective terms refer cannot readily be specified by the elemental categories (above), many modern philosophers at least tacitly acknowledge that these terms may characterize key *relationships* among what have been referred to here as elemental categories.

Chief among these nonobjective concepts is the notion of *role* introduced in the last chapter. Although not properly an elemental category, role is nevertheless an essential feature in our theory of coercion. In making this assertion this chapter veers from its heretofore empirical course, for despite the empirically verifiable correlates associated with *role*, it is largely a subjective (and intersubjective) notion and ultimately may function as a linkage term between the subjective and objective aspects in the larger theory. Furthermore, role mediates the empirical categories of individuals and actions through a reexamination of their participation in a dynamic power-and-control relationship. It is by virtue of the concept of role that coercion is a relational phenomenon.

While on the surface the idea of a linkage term may be compelling, on closer analysis, *role* is a complex concept. Its blending of diverse philosophical approaches leads us to question how subjective and objective criteria can be systematically combined into a unified social theory. While precedents for combining such criteria are not difficult to cite, few authors have accomplished this without compromising either the subjective or the empirical status of their project at the outset.

This chapter will be directed towards establishing an epistemological foundation for the theory of coercion, particularly in consideration of the concept of role. A preliminary section will document the usage of what may tentatively be called nonobjective variables of coercion. A discussion of these variables as they have been approached in the philosophical literature on coercion will include an examination of the (acknowledged or unacknowledged) subjective aspects of each variable in the context of attempts to reconcile them to a predominantly empirical viewpoint.

Following the discussion of the subjective correlates of coercion, the concept of intersubjectivity will be introduced. This section will include precedents for an understanding of intersubjectivity in social philosophy as well as the preferred meaning of the term in the present context. It is my assertion that the notion of intersubjectivity, most systematically developed within phenomenological treatises, can contribute substantially to an understanding of *role* and in turn, to the relational nature of coercion. Although no claim is being pressed that we approach our analysis from a phenomenological point of view, we acknowledge that there are subjective and intersubjective concerns central to the concept of role that may be formulated with reference to phenomenology and the social sciences. Ultimately in the following chapters, I will seek to show that intersubjectivity provides an epistemological grounding to the concept of role and that phenomenological insights can elucidate certain power, freedom, and autonomy relations in the coercive event.

To that eventual purpose, the final sections of the chapter will approach role theory as it relates to our view of coercion. Our examination of each of the nonobjective variables from an inter-subjective perspective should demonstrate the analytical power and impact of a relational view of coercion. By identifying the appropriate role relationships with which each intersubjective variable is associated, subjective facets may be correlated with the empirical categories of participants and behaviors.

NONOBJECTIVE REFERENCES IN EMPIRICAL
THEORIES OF COERCION

In framing their definitions of coercion, most philosophers choose a predominantly empirical approach. However, the view that coercion consists of a certain set of control relationships does not readily lend itself to an empirical treatment. In addition to the quantifiable, observable phenomena (such as actors, agents, and their physical behaviors) essential to considerations of coercion, there are also nonphysical and/or affective properties and events (such as reasons, motives, wants, and intentions), as well as intersubjective meanings conveyed among the participants. Indeed, the subjective meaning that one participant holds for the other or the perspective from which one views the other can, in some cases, make the difference in the identification of a given relation as an instance of coercion. Hence nonobjective factors must be given a proper and full accounting by a social theory that purports to include all relevant and significant influences on the social phenomenon under study.

Some of the philosophical treatments mentioned in the preceding chapter have also alluded to the relational aspects of coercion. Yet even those writers that openly acknowledge the existence of role relationships have usually employed an objective format in which the objective, subjective and intersubjective features of coercion are treated with an even hand. Some writers, notably Felix Oppenheim whose theory is discussed in the next chapter, offer an instrumentalized treatment of many abstract concepts. This type of instrumentalized approach to social phenomena avoids references to the subjective structures of groups and individuals. Accordingly, the success or failure of such attempts largely depend upon how well abstract relational ideas can be reduced to empirical or quantifiable behavior.

Other objectivists, in recognition of the existence of subjective aspects in coercion, may attempt merely to introduce 'nonobjective terms' into their definitions. However, this approach is ultimately unsatisfactory in part because it cannot get to the 'meanings' that the interactive relations may have for the participants themselves. As a matter of principle, the objectivist must restrict his account of social relations involving human actors and interrelationships to those aspects of behavior that are public and observable to the objectivist. Each of the following examples of recent philosophical definitions of coercion contains references to nonobjective phenomena, as presented within an empirical format. (I have underlined key 'nonobjective' terms essential to the definition so they may be easily identified by the reader.)

Virginia Held claims that coercion occurs "where the person coerced did what he did against his will"; that is, it is the activity of causing or enabling someone to do something against his or her will that is characteristic of coercion. The notion of *will* is also central to Dauenhauer's definition of coercion: "the use of techniques and physical implements to impose one's *will* upon another." According to Gunderson, coercion is the use of or the threat of the use of force *against the permission* of the victim. In other words, the victim either fails or refuses to give *consent* to the coercer for the implied coerced action. Mark Fowler claims that "coercion always involves a definite agent (a specific individual or organization) *intentionally* threatening some other definite agent for the purpose of eliciting a definite action." As unintentional or prudential imperatives would not be considered by Fowler as instruments of coercion, 'deliberateness' is a key feature or 'root-concept' of his definition. Elsewhere in his article Fowler introduces further nonempirical references as he states that "coercion invariably involves imposing a practical imperative on someone, leaving him no *reasonable choice* but to perform the coerced deed." A variation on Fowler's definition is offered by Bernard Gert who sees coercion as the "result of a threat of evil which provides an *unreasonable* incentive." Patrick Wilson expresses both a definition of coercion and practical criteria for determining whether a particular set of circumstances is to be viewed as an instance of coercion; in his formulation, an instance of coercion may be recognized as such by determining whether "people for whatever reason (right or wrong), resist the application of physical or psychological force or the threat of it to make them act *against their wishes* or prevent them from *doing what they want.*" In this view, coercion has to do with overcoming resistance by force, that is, in cases where some resistance is conceivable or possible. Frankfurt claims that, in coercion, the victim is made to do some action by being given "a certain type of *motive* for doing so." Finally we note the definition of Michael Taylor who sees a threat as coercive if it elicits compliance and does so "by proposing a sanction which the recipient *expects* to be imposed" for noncompliance.[1]

As the rest of this chapter is devoted to an elaboration of the subjective and intersubjective aspects of coercion from a nonempirical perspective, some prefatory remarks will be made about each of the abstract terms, as underlined above. Each term will be introduced as it has been approached empirically, and a brief statement will be made about its nonobjective character.

NONOBJECTIVE TERMS FROM AN EMPIRICAL POINT OF VIEW

Will: The term 'will' is basically an abstraction for one's disposition, capacity, or power to effect a reason or to determine an action. In the context of coercion, it is an activity term that relates to a mental event of deciding or choosing to (or not to) do something. While the activity of willing may or may not culminate in observable behavior, the objective character of Q's doing q or being coerced to do q implies that to *any* observer, including P, it is evident that Q does q. However, in real situations it cannot be evident in the same immediate way to any observer that q is performed against Q's will. For what may or may not have been contrary to Q's disposition (at a specific time, according to circumstances) is a matter internal to Q (i.e., it is a mental state of Q) unless Q has unequivocally and publicly communicated to others the nature of his disposition with respect to q. Thus 'will' must be considered to be a nonobjective term even though it is used as an essential feature in certain empirical definitions of coercion.[2] It is important to note that no matter to what extent that the concept of will may be operationalized, it postulates the influence of certain subjective states upon certain objective relations and actions.

Consent, Permission: These terms are central to a number of definitions of coercion[3] and also appear to be used interchangeably. Because the only apparent difference between them is for our purposes negligible—where 'permission' indicates a more formal authorization and 'consent' indicates an expression of the subject's affirmation or willingness (and is, perhaps, the more general of the two terms)—all references in what follows will be to 'consent'.

'Consent' has been construed in objective terms. To discern what makes 'consent' objective in certain definitions, take the following. It has been claimed that coercion is eliminated only if the recipient of force willingly grants permission ('consent') at the time each act of force is applied, and, in addition, this view argues that actual communication of Q's, the recipient's, (un)willingness or consent is immaterial to a consideration of the coercive nature of the act.[4] (This is evidently intended to cover cases in which Q cannot or may not communicate his dissent, perhaps for reasons of circumstance, incapacity, or prudence). An objective treatment will generally emphasize the observable, public character of acts that communicate Q's consent, but it will also accommodate judgments based on probability or equivalence, in the absence of explicit behavioral expressions of consent. Accordingly, Q's 'tacit consent' in doing Q may presumably be objectifiable if it is held to have been done without any visible sign of dissent and/or over time.

In practice it is not always possible to distinguish on objective grounds between 'tacit' or uncommunicated consent and implicit dissent or one's actions and the subjective reasons, values, beliefs, etc. one may have for taking those actions. The view stated above with respect to 'consent' is not thoroughly objective insofar as it presupposes the subjective presence of consent as being a crucial determinant of the coerciveness of (P's) action, besides its various explicit public forms. Even the forms considered most objective must be regarded as subjective in origin, but they must also be regarded as involving the inner process of appraisal, judgment, and, perhaps, execution, in the manner of an externalizing (or communicative) act of will. Consequently, although the term consent appears in otherwise 'objective' definitions of coercion, it is basically a nonobjective term that may be expressed empirically.

Intentions, Motives: In claiming that P and Q had certain 'motives' in doing p and q respectively, we mean that P and Q had a certain mental or subjective state or belief that caused, or is the reason for, moving their 'wills' and impelling the actions they performed. Motives are viewed operationally from the standpoint of actions that are supposed to have been done on their behalf. The term 'intention' may refer to the object towards which one's thoughts are directed or to a determination to do something, perhaps in a certain manner, regardless of whether in either case it leads to an action or to an action done deliberately. Objectively, the imputation of specific 'intentions' in individual cases is always a matter of interpretation based on circumstantial evidence and logical extrapolation unless the parties concerned clearly express them. P may coerce Q intentionally or may be motivated to coerce Q, but neither P's (and Q's) intention or motive in this regard is observable in the same way as P's (and Q's) action is. We see that in some cases relating to a question of coercion, P's threat, p, may be intended to bring about Q's doing q, but Q, in doing q, may not have had the motive P intended Q to have.

Since 'intention' and/or 'motive' are terms that figure importantly in some empirical definitions of coercion, we shall cite an example of an attempt to objectify 'motive' as it is found in the writings of Gert when he states that rational persons will avoid a significant evil and that this serves as a 'motive' for all rational persons.[5] However, in practice, the general ascription of motive 'Z' to 'all rational persons' is not of much help in particular cases in which the identification of a specific motive behind Q's doing q is necessary for determining the coerciveness of the action. So long as the subjective states and mental objects (ideas) that constitute motives and intentions continue to influence and explain human

behavior, the essentially nonobjective character of 'motives' and
'intentions' must be given their proper representation in attempts at
their objectification.

Wants, Needs, Wishes, Desires: Found in some definitions of
coercion, these terms generally refer to certain subjective realities
that are treated as 'observables' in a figurative or abstract sense
only. As personally 'real' as they are to us, 'needs', 'wants',
'wishes', and 'desires' are never actually 'observables' like the
objective modes of behavior meant to fulfill them are. For
example, as X dines, we observe X's activity, but we do not literally
perceive X's *need* for nutrition being satisfied; indeed, from this
viewpoint 'need' is an abstraction. Yet we *understand* the basic
existential necessity behind X's behavior in general, despite a
variety of approaches X might utilize towards this end. Objectively,
needs, wants, desires, and so on appear to be indistinguishable,
except by abstraction, from the behaviors they ostensibly express.
Granted, some 'needs' originate in our biology, somes 'wishes' in
our univeral psychic unconscious, and some 'wants' from society,
but the objective side of their beginnings and behavioral modes of
disclosure does not exhaust the concretely experienced 'fullness' of
their status as living events in our inner subjective lives. In the equal
objectification of all their main component elements, some
definitions of coercion overlook this crucial nonobjective
dimension of 'needs', and so on. The unavoidable implication, as I
see it, for the objectivist approach to defining coercion is that
unless Q's 'wishes', 'desires', and so on, are somehow self-evident
or clearly embedded in the actions or self-revelations being
observed, a determination of coercion cannot be made by a mere
application of a definition to a situation that allegedly exemplifies
it on a one-to-one correspondence basis.

Choice: The role of the term 'choice' in various definitions of
coercion is very important because its presence in a certain social
relation is meant to determine both the existence and degree of its
coerciveness. Where Q has 'no choice but' to do the coerced deed,
q, marks the *existence* of coercion; and where Q 'chooses' to do q
rather than face the 'evils' threatened by the coercer suggests the
degree to which Q is coerced. The phrase 'no choice but' (i.e., Q
had 'no choice but' to yield to P's threat) does not necessarily mean
'no choice whatsoever' but rather 'no reasonable choice.'

The 'act of choosing' or 'making a choice' is a mental event. It refers to a voluntary mental act (or event) of selecting that which is preferred from among at least two or more alternatives (things, courses of action, even perhaps, one's attitude towards something). The implicit criterion of reasonableness of choice as to whether and to what extent coercion has occurred is a common device used for objectifying a series of prior events which presumably culminate in Q's doing q. In simplified form, with respect to P, Q moves from 'having a choice' to 'making a choice', and then to 'acting on the choice made'. Objectively, it may be seen that Q has done q. But whether observable action, q, is the result of any degree of choice on Q's part cannot be decided entirely on this ground alone unless Q acknowledges that this is so. The blanks in the objective format are filled in by an appeal to a hypothetical rational observer who calculates a set of 'reasonable' behavioral expectations and explanations for 'persons under a given set of circumstances'. Hence, we learn more about the rational conditions and features of observation from the criterion of reasonableness than about what may or may not have occurred subjectively in Q's internal process of decision-making. But since this nonobjective factor is indispensable to a consideration of all relevant factors influencing Q's response to P, an empirical definition that misrepresents 'choice' is deficient.

Expectation: By the term 'expectation' we ordinarily mean that a person looks forward to, anticipates, or believes that something will occur. The phenomenon of 'expectancy' can be associated with certain physical behaviors. In addition, the 'something' to which it refers may have an empirical status (such as a steak, movie, or a certain income). In fact, the objectivist approaches 'expectation' solely in terms of the aforementioned 'observables' in an effort to deny or 'objectify' its subjectivity. When Q is said to 'expect' to be the recipient of certain sanctions for not conforming to P's demand, 'expectation' plays a significant causal role in Q's deciding to do the coerced action; indeed, it may be the centrally relevant motive in Q's doing q. The objectivist is committed to a translation of 'expectation' into the language of objectivity once it is accepted that a person's 'expectations' are causally efficacious. In cases like coercion, however, Q's inner expectation may not at all coincide with Q's actual behavior; nor does it share the same

objective status as other 'observables': participants P and Q.
Nevertheless, those who insist on defining coercion empirically also
tend to treat all its various features, including nonobjective ones
such as 'expectation', as if they are objectifiable.

Again let me point out that I have no objection to definitions
that use such terms as 'will', 'choice', 'consent', and so on, for
such notions are critical concepts in a thorough treatment of
coercion. Empirical definitions of coercion have typically pressed
into service these nonobjective terms for their useful insights into
certain aspects of coercion that are not empirically verifiable. As
nonobjective terms they may often be understood as 'subjective',
meaning present *only* in the 'inner life' of an actor(s) as are
intersubjective phenomena. Alternately, they may merely have
important subjective facets, referring to 'contents of
consciousness' such as specific mental or affective states or
personal or private matters known only to those actors concerned.
While these 'contents of consciousness' may eventually build to
decisions, commitments, behaviors, or actions that are, in turn,
objectifiable as subjective (or pre-objective) states, a proposition
that asserts its own existence is neither true nor false in the ordinary
sense, and it otherwise prohibits measurement or quantification.

Ultimately, these nonobjective terms as outlined above may have
both objective and subjective meanings, but in a theory of coercion
they are equivocal unless these different senses are distinguished.
Unfortunately, the failure to provide an epistemological grounding
for these abstract terms occurs all too frequently, creating a serious
impediment to a thoroughgoing grasp of coercion as a social
relation. Further, it is also necessary to suggest that social science is
perhaps not best suited to an epistemology such as empiricism that
may be more ideally reserved for the natural sciences. The
distinctive character of social reality often harmonizes with the
application of nonempirical modes of discovery and analysis, for
example, the interpretative or hermeneutic type.

INTERSUBJECTIVITY

In the preceding section each nonobjective term as drawn from
various definitions of coercion has been represented with respect to
its typical portrayal in traditional philosophical empiricism. While

alluding to certain drawbacks inherent in these types of treatments, I have nevertheless maintained that the mere reference to unobservable or subjective features should not in itself disparage the integrity of an empirical approach. If certain factors are taken into account, it is possible for subjective phenomena to be explained within an empirical framework.

However, one might assert that the empirical approach leaves us only with the following possibilities, none of which preserves the truly subjective character of the phenomena to which we refer:

1. an inference to unobservable subjective reality based on an interpretation of overt behavior;
2. a dismissal of the inner mental life as having any causal influence on behavior;
3. an embrace of external behavior as forming the essence of 'subjective' terminology:

Body events and environmental events are thus seen to be the only causes of behavior.

In many studies of the social world, it is commonly claimed that role structure shapes a person's concept of the 'self' and of the 'other'; moreover, role is taken as central to the nature and function of interactive behaviors. It allows us to account for facets of reality that are at once subjective and empirically understandable.

The concept of role that in turn receives its foundation in the theory of intersubjectivity is central to this account of coercion; it provides a linkage between the subjective and objective domains characterized in some accounts as discrete realms. (Intersubjectivity radically diverges from pure empiricism concerning its depiction of the *standpoint* from which knowledge of social reality is acquired.) The intersubjective approach assumes a close relationship between the 'observer' and the social world being observed. This assumption refers to the basic mode in which all persons (including the scientific 'observer') experience the world in a normal continuum of experiences as a shared world populated by other similarly experiencing beings. Thus, if much of intersubjective experience of the self and relations with others can be construed in terms of role or role structures, the concept of role can be used to account for our knowledge of others—if not in their independent uniqueness that only they can know, then as 'subjects' and 'objects' of experience.

The concept of intersubjectivity has received a wide variety of meanings and applications in philosophical history. A concise overview of the various interpretations of the term may serve to clarify the sense in which it is taken for the present analysis of coercion. Although I do not approach intersubjectivity from a phenomenological viewpoint, one must acknowledge the contributions of Alfred Schutz and other phenomenologists, whose insights have spawned more versatile treatments of related issues in social philosophy. Accordingly, the concepts denoted here as 'subjective terms' because of their sometimes awkward and ungrounded associations in purely empirical accounts can be reconciled in the intersubjective approach. Through a theory of intersubjectivity, nonempirical, mental idealizations can be accounted for without compromising the objective status of empirically verifiable phenomena.

HISTORY OF INTERSUBJECTIVITY

Intersubjectivity is a philosophical notion that has been raised as a question or problem by many philosophers, both classical[6] and modern, from within their respective traditions. As a question it has taken the form of how 'knowledge of other minds' is possible. As a problem, it involves attempts at certifiable propositions about the existential status of 'other minds'. By contrast, there are philosophical perspectives that trivialize 'intersubjectivity' owing to their rejection of a belief in 'private mental substance'. There are still others who advance the claim that without an awareness of the fact of our intersubjective life and experiences we would not be able to conceive of ourselves as 'persons', that is, as valuing, reasoning, willing, and self-acting beings.

There are at least two older significant cognitive views on intersubjectivity: the rationalistic and the empiricistic. Neither one of these conveys quite the same meaning of intersubjectivity employed in the present theory of coercion, but a succinct statement about each should offer some relevant insights into the notion of intersubjectivity and its evolution.

RATIONALISTIC VIEW OF INTERSUBJECTIVITY

The most important and perhaps the first expression of the difficulties associated with intersubjectivity is found in the writings of the early philosophical rationalist René Descartes (1596-1650). In his quest for certain knowledge (i.e., for ideas whose truth can be known with certainty), he claims to have certified by distinctly rational methods the existence of two separate irreducible substances: physical body substance and mind substance.[7] Human beings are known to be distinct unions of body and mind. But, since no clearly rational idea reveals to him how it is possible for events in each separate realm of reality to influence or cause events in the other (which common sense and self observation suggest to occur not infrequently), a metaphysical dichotomy was noted in Descartes' philosophy that became known as the classical "Mind-Body Problem."

Accordingly, for the Cartesian Rationalist, intersubjectivity emerges in the effort to establish the metaphysical basis for the apparent interaction between minds and bodies. Specifically, the rationalist attempts to explain the epistemology behind how 'I' appear to 'myself' in a union between body and mind as the ground for how others appear to 'myself' as beings whose bodies and minds are inextricably linked (despite that the first-hand knowledge of the existence of the other's mind is absolutely private and unknowable from anyone else's viewpoint). For the classical Cartesian, as for modern defenders of metaphysical dualism, 'intersubjectivity' involves rationally acquired knowledge that other selves have minds like one's own; this knowledge is held to exist for each individual despite the exclusivity of one's access to inner mental processes. Personal knowledge of the identity of others as 'selves' is seen as being acquired through an extension of one's own self knowledge: through the process of thinking certain privileged thoughts. In addition, it is consistent with rationalism that the identities of 'selves' or 'persons' as singular unions of bodies and minds is conceived on an individualistic level, unrelated to the question of the prior existence or the intersubjective influences of the 'society of other selves'. Thus, for rationalism, the concept of self identity is conceived independently of the social world. In short, the 'person' is a union of body and mind in which are contained certain preconceived ideas about the nature and reality of self- or person-hood. In this view, there is an innateness of reason so that observation will bear out what the self already knows.

CLASSICAL EMPIRICAL VIEW
OF INTERSUBJECTIVITY

Classical empiricism, as expressed in the works of its leading representative, David Hume (1711-1776), is a rejection of the earlier rationalistic theories of knowledge and reality. Particularly, empiricism refutes the Cartesian concept of self-identity and with it, the problem of intersubjectivity that is held to arise owing to the postulate of a mind-body dualism. Instead, the cardinal empiricist principle of epistemology is that all cognitive knowledge of reality has its origins not in pre-formed self-certified ideas but in perceptual experience. Hume denies that mind or selfhood are substantive. Rather he characterized the mind as a bundle of sensations or experiences at the center of one's attention; what one's experience reports is a certain relation between ideas that the imagination inclines to unite into a composite.[8] The fate of the problem of intersubjectivity rests on the empiricists' criterion for forming a belief in the existence of mind, namely, perception. Any intersubjective possibility of reciprocal influence between persons in their conscious awareness is explainable (or reducible) solely and ultimately on the basis of perceptual experience. Thus, from the empirical viewpoint of Hume, we are told nothing in principle about the pre-perceptual historical and social influences on our perceptions (i.e., how we have come to perceive ourselves and our world as we do) or about the principles that account for our perceptions of ourselves as 'persons' or communities of persons. These considerations, important as they are for our present concept of intersubjectivity, are beyond the scope of Hume's empiricism.

PROBLEMS IN THE COGNITIVE VIEW OF
INTERSUBJECTIVITY

Whatever enduring and numerous insights these early philosophies may have contributed to the concept of intersubjectivity, the plethora of modern criticism that has been directed towards them is centered on at least one telling consideration. The concept of intersubjectivity becomes a chief difficulty whenever it is required of the experiencing subject to give an account of others who are experienced as beings with their own centers of experience and to account for them wholly from his or her own experiential or egological standpoint of reference. It is true that early rationalism and empiricism did not exactly claim that "cognitive consciousness is the universal condition of being," which has been correctly recognized as the cardinal principle of many forms of idealism; however, there is something of an "egocentric predicament"[9] when the problem of intersubjectivity is a consequence, either in its acceptance or rejection as such, of defining all knowledge and reality in terms of the self alone or through the unrestricted use of a single method.[10] Accordingly, one is inclined to indict various contemporary views on intersubjectivity for encountering the same difficulty; yet, by no means do I suggest that this is the most revealing criticism against some contemporary views, for each carries its own additional strengths and weaknesses. Neither of these need detain us here.

Although early empiricism denies the problem of intersubjectivity, some later modern forms of empiricist objectivism of the analytic or linguistic varitety not only acknowledge a 'problem' along this vein but attempt its resolution based on certain inductive and deductive arguments believed to be consistent with empirical experimental inquiry.[11] The issue for them is whether sense experience provides sufficient grounds for justifying a belief in the existence of other minds. Intersubjectivity concerns, then, not so much what observables indicate about what is going on in someone else's inner life but rather what empirical evidential basis there is for believing that anything is going on at all. The most common strategy used by some philosophers of empiricism is to propose either an inductive or analogical argument as a solution to the problem of intersubjectivity. Based on the observation-supported generalization that "certain properties have been found to be conjoined in various contexts" (e.g., one's own body, feelings, and conscious awareness of one's self as a succession of feelings, and so on), the inductive inference is drawn that "in a further context, the conjunction will hold," that is, with respect to other's bodies being conjoined to feelings, and so forth. What one observes to be true in one's own case (i.e., from the inside out, as it were) is an alternative analogical paradigm for knowledge about the inner existence of other minds. In this view, 'observables' such as behavior, first person utterances, and circumstances may be seen as 'evidence' or even criteria for claims about 'unobservable' other minds.[12]

These recent forms or logical empiricism—and the earlier forms as well (namely, Hume's and J. S. Mill's)—share at least this much in common as concerns 'intersubjectivity', and so, to this extent, they suffer the same error: a basic misconception about the relation between the observer and the observed—that is, that intersubjectivity is (or is not) an epistemological problem because the passive, isolated observer is unable to 'receive' information about unobservables (such as motives, intentions, and other inner phenomena of other minds) through sensory stimulation by external inputs. Furthermore, it may be that the phenomenon of intersubjectivity can be understood differently on a noncognitive or affective level. This hypothesis offers a significant contemporary alternative account to the primarily cognitive treatments exemplified by the various types of rationalism and empiricism already discussed.

NONCOGNITIVE VIEW OF INTERSUBJECTIVITY

In a noncognitive handling of intersubjectivity, it is not necessary to make logical inferences from one's own observations to those of others: the interior affective or unobservable states of others are known immediately and naturally. The other's bodily existence is never experienced by oneself as a primordial datum, but, rather, the other's body is already given as embodiment of mental life.[13] It is experienced as a 'lived body' and as the other self's expression of its own inner life center. What is expressed in the eyes of the other is known immediately, naturally, and noncognitively.[14]

The power of this insight may often be short-circuited when generalizations are applied in some specific cases. However, in those instances where knowledge of other minds is unmediated and self-evident, the problem of intersubjectivity vanishes and with it the necessity for resolving through various 'proofs' that other minds exist and are knowable.[15] In other words, if intersubjective knowledge is not taken as a matter of representation or cognition, then cognitive proofs or rational demonstrations of correctness are not required since the 'truth' of such claims are manifest or axiomatic.

On balance, whatever 'truths' may be expressed through this approach to intersubjectivity,[16] they are quite easily undermined by an arbitrary, irrationalistic point of departure that is ultimately incompatible with a scientific perspective. No single claim can be any more or less supportable than any other, for what one sees in another's eyes may not be seen by all observers. Thus the universality of observation that is necessary to scientific claims is lacking as well as the set of procedural safeguards that are characteristic of scientific self-correction. Hence, in this type of noncognitive treatment of intersubjectivity, there does not appear to be a rational check on the veracity of claims, as these are taken to be self-evident.

On the other hand, not all noncognitive approaches to intersubjectivity are ultimately incompatible with the scientific point of view. Generally, the noncognitive approaches do us the important services of focusing our attention on other primary features of human existence (namely, the conative and the affective) besides those that are derivative of pure cognitivism. In my view, the noncognitive approach most fully captures the 'sense' of intersubjectivity in our everyday lives but only insofar as it does not preclude the participation of scientific observation in its method of inquiry.

Some further philosophical observations about intersubjectivity are in order before approaching the subjective and objective theoretical terms of coercion from an intersubjective perspective. First, I think that we are correct in our assertion that intersubjectivity is a universal human condition. As human organisms we attempt to orient, structure, and live our lives not exclusively in accordance with the abilities and accomplishments of our cognitive powers. It is also true that the volitional and affective processes of our cognitive lives incline us towards other living organisms like ourselves. Thus, there is, I believe, a powerful pre-cognitive sense in which we are and become conscious of others' and our own engagement in a preexisting social world.

However, the acknowledgment of this noncognitive *awareness* is not to diminish the participation and contributions of cognitive consciousness to our intersubjective *understanding* of our world, nor is it to suggest that intersubjective existence is accessible exclusively or even adequately through noncognitive consciousness. It is merely to indicate that, in a most profound sense, all human knowledge and social theory is always preceded by a more basic openness, directedness, or awareness towards others. Our lives have a conscious, intersubjective meaning even as we attempt to understand this condition of human life. The source of intersubjective meaning lies in the affective dimension of our communicative encounter with others like ourselves. The 'we-relation' between ourselves and others is the core of our own self-awareness as persons. As we respond to being affected by others and so seek reciprocally to open ourselves communicatively in everyday encounters, we already are in possession of an intersubjective awareness at the root of all our daily endeavors.

SUMMARY OF THE NONCOGNITIVE APPROACH TO INTERSUBJECTIVITY

The noncognitive approach to intersubjectivity that I support denies that our social identities as 'persons' is (a) basically a conceptual construction that is 'built up' in our consciousness from isolated, rudimentary units of experience, (b) a preconceived innate idea revealed to our inner awareness, and (c) simply an empirically observable social fact. It also rejects various 'irrationalist' claims and forms of noncognitivism, for example, that the other person's inner life in its particular 'states' or 'contexts' at any specific time can be understood immediately and naturally with self-evident certainty. Finally, it rejects the view that our minds bring to experience, a priori, an intersubjective or social framework understanding all interrelationships between persons.[17]

What I hold as supportable about noncognitivism and intersubjectivity may be summarized in the following propositions:

1. Intersubjectivity is a universal condition of human existence. Our reflection on the totality of human experience suggests that this is so.

2. In face-to-face encounters we experience others not merely as material bodies but as lived bodies or 'body subjects'. Internal experiential processing involves a combination of sensory inputs and interpreted

meanings that forms our intersubjective awareness of the other and the social world.

3. Intersubjectivity then should not be considered as a 'problem', as it has been viewed traditionally. Most of what we do and are in our everyday lives is explainable in terms of our awareness of belonging to a common world, shared by others like ourselves. As I understand it, 'intersubjectivity' does not stand or fall on the dispensable issue of whether it can be *shown* that others have minds or specific thoughts at any given time.

THE PHENOMENON OF ROLE

In order to analyze coercion, we must first acknowledge that social relations and actions are derived from a certain set of evolving social structures. Keeping in mind what has just been said about intersubjectivity, we turn our attention to the phenomenon of social role. In our discussion we have briefly touched on 'social role' as a factor in the dynamic and relational character of coercion. A basic unit in sociological analysis, the concept of role is applied here to explain (1) why certain relationships become coercive; (2) that certain actions are coercive because they forge a coercive relationship between the participants (that cannot be comprehended merely with reference to the subjective states of the participants); and (3) that some relations and actions are coercive owing to 'internalized' roles and other nonobjective aspects of role relations.

If we view 'role' as a basic social concept in terms of which human interactive relations may be elucidated, then an appeal to role becomes necessary for an accurate and productive depiction of coercion as a social phenomenon. It is not enough to say that only actions may be coercive or, conversely, that coercion can be understood only in terms of related actions. It is important to acknowledge that social actions occur in a relational context of which coercion is one possible outcome. Thus, relationships can also be coercive. In those cases, the role aspect of the relationship may offer the best insight into its coercive character.

Roles are relationships that help us to structure social relational contexts both as participants and observers. Certainly not all coercive relations are founded in role relations that are *predominantly* coercive. However, it is evident that to understand the actions and types of relations that are *potentially* coercive, we require an analytical framework that takes into account both the empirical correlates of social relations as well as our intersubjective comprehension of the contexts in which such relations occur. To review, it is the intersubjective approach to role that shows the intelligible unity of these different factors of social coercion.

As we began our discussion, it is best to formulate a definition of role and to observe the social contexts in which roles occur. Parenthetically, our discussion of role will be continued in the following chapters where it will be reintroduced into an empirical framework of analysis. This treatment eventually builds towards an exposition of the dynamic character of coercion, for the degree of coerciveness in any given relationship may fluctuate as a function of certain role changes that occur naturally among the participants. Thus, some relations may be intrinsically coercive, whereas others may develop noncoercively, gradually acquire coercive aspects, and, later perhaps, lose them again.

SOCIAL CONTEXTS OF ROLE: INDIVIDUALS AND GROUPS

It is a common and basic fact of the social world of persons that we understand and conduct most of our relations with others in terms of a complex of social roles. On the interpersonal level, role relations and role behavior are commonplace. Roles take myriad forms, many with labels such as Banker, Teacher, Parent, or Employer. Sometimes the roles we play involve us in joining certain groups. Conversely, we also discover that the groups in which we hold membership cast us in roles related to the group's nature and purpose. Furthermore, as each of us may hold multiple memberships in various sorts of groups, our behavior and even our relationships may reflect or be a consequence of such membership, deriving their 'meaning' for both participants and observers from these various sources. Indeed, sometimes we have internalized our membership in groups to the point that such membership becomes a vital aspect of our self-identities. Thus, some people do not merely belong to the Republican Party: they *are* Republicans. On the other hand, membership in the group of public transportation ridership is less frequently internalized.

The extent to which roles become internalized is related to how they are structured or defined within a group or interpersonal context. There are tightly structured roles like those formulated in job descriptions; the social relations that are composed of such roles are correspondingly well structured. Loosely defined roles may not be as easily identified because they are less uniform or repetitive.

In a group context the type and degree of role structure can be a reflection of the internal organization of the group itself. Some groups are formally organized (e.g., with a basic charter, statement of purpose, and so on) while others are less so. Some groups have voluntary membership that may be renounced or refused while in others, membership may not be open to personal election (e.g., the unemployed, the sick, the conscriptible). (So too with general abstractions like membership in the human species. In this case those who believe that the human species is a social group do so primarily because the social, civilized community feature of human nature implies a purpose in view of which humans organize themselves into closely or less closely knit structures.) With some groups we can be active members; with others our membership is in name only.

Our behavior may deliberately reflect or get its 'meaning' from our group affiliation to the degree we are consciously aware of belonging to and identifying with a particular group or believe our membership imposes certain responsibilities or attitudes. It is also the case that sometimes we are treated or categorized as if we belong to or have chosen to belong to a certain group that we disvalue.

Group organization and function may in turn derive and alter its 'meaning' from differing behaviors of its individual members. For example, each and every member of a political party may not hold the same views with respect to the party line. Yet each member considers himself or herself as part of the larger group, participating with others in a role relationship that may fluctuate in its expression. Accordingly, the party line as a function of these relationships may be viewed as a changing, inconsistent grouping of positions on various issues.

Whether a particular group is formally or informally organized and whether its composite roles are tightly or loosely defined, invariably there are recognized criteria for group membership. Further, many groups have assigned or naturally accrued a certain set of rights and obligations for all members. These may stipulate penalities for disrespect, and, in extreme cases, excommunication from the group may be mandated. On the other hand, some groups affix no penalities for violations either because there is an unavoidable vagueness about the specific rights and duties accruing to membership, or because no enforcement mechanism is available. For example, the World Court may 'find' against a member of the international community, but it can do nothing except publicize its 'finding'. In terms of membership, group size may have some bearing on the group's importance relative to other groups and to the priority it receives. Conflict situations often arise among group-claims; in vying for a member's response, respect for membership in one group may supercede allegiance to another group's 'pull'.

DEFINITION OF ROLE: OBJECTIVE AND SUBJECTIVE CORRELATES

From an empirical standpoint, 'role' may be seen as a prescribed and organized pattern of behavior (or social function) that correlates with an actor's status in a particular situation, operation, process, or society. Accordingly, role can be viewed as both a social datum and as a unit of social scientific analysis. It is an abstraction meant to explain organized and repeatable behaviors along with their corresponding social functions. We will discuss in due course how this definition might be modified in accordance with an inter-subjective perspective.

Objectively defined roles or aspects of roles such as those exemplified in formal job descriptions typify the abstract set of expectations publicly conveyed by employers to prospective employees. In keeping with this example, job specifications look to empirically verifiable correlates of the employment experience by indicating the tasks, skills, and often the attitudes needed or expected for one to perform acceptably on the job so described. Job descriptions may be tightly structured and assume written form, unequivocally spelling out the rights and duties of the job. Insofar as such descriptions can be construed as a typification of a role relationship, a compatible, objectivistic definition of role might be "a cluster of rights and duties with some sort of social function." In a similar vein, 'role' can be seen as "repeatable patterns of social relations . . . structured partly by the rules of . . . socially acceptable behavior."[18] In short, definitions that approach 'role' through an observation of rule-governed patterns of social behavior conform to an objective mode of inquiry that is effective insofar as such manifest patterns, behaviors, or actions are objectifiable.

A prominent drawback of this approach to 'role' is its one-dimensional nature. It overlooks the actors' own experienced social reality that does not *uniformly* coincide with an empirically specified set of behaviors. The job specifications as formally presented may not be an *exact* representation of the expectations of either the employer or the employee. As a tightly structured and objectified portrayal of a 'cluster of rights and duties' associated with an actual or potential role relationship, the job specification serves an important function for the 'employer' and 'employee' and for the larger society that assigns them their identity. However, the job specification does not portray the actual or anticipated *experience* of the lived role relationship.

Thus, there are clearly some behaviors or relationships between actors for which an objective methodology is inappropriate. For example, in realizing a mental plan of his own creation, an actor joins or interacts with others on the basis of the prescriptive requirements of the plan. His behavior and social relations as they become patterned in accord with the plan are essentially role-structured. The actor plays these out in the process of 'plan' realization, and it is only with respect to the 'plan' that the 'role' nature is established. Many people attend college for the single purpose of acquiring the degree that will help them land the job for which their education is supposed to prepare them. The daily relationships, pursuits, and activities of these students become meaningful ultimately as they are related to career 'plans'. In some cases this is the only source of their meaning or coherency. Playing the role of student is objective to the extent that it follows the prescription of matriculation. It is subjective or, perhaps, intersubjective, as the mental plan explains, guides, or determines the behaviors and relationships recommended by it. The 'role' and the 'plan' are rendered no less subjective if ultimately the objective plan goal is met by the student in assuming his designated career orientation.

Subjective aspects of roles are evident in cases where 'actors' project their own mental plans or life projects into the social landscape in which they seek to realize them. As a note of caution, the term 'subjective' as it is used here is not meant to carry such connotations as 'impressionistic', 'arbitrary', or 'irrational'. The subjective processes underlying the decisions of an 'actor' may be utterly logical, intelligible, and even predictable as they evolve in accord with a personal, mental plan. That such subjectively derived aspects of roles are not directly knowable to another individual does not render them any less influential than their objective correlates. Indeed, we acknowledge the subjective frame of reference to role behavior through such expressions as 'intentions', 'choices', 'expectations' and other nonobjective events of an actor's mental life. Whenever such terms intrude into an empirical social theory, one cannot ignore that the very fact of their presence is testimony to the realization that without them interactions and social relations would be incomprehensible. An actor is also a thinker.

One might argue, then, that subjectively *defined* aspects of roles should be included along with objective factors in a general account of 'social role' (a concept we hold to be a necessary feature in a theory of coercion). Actions and relations linked to social roles may receive their ultimate meaning from the subjective source that calls forth the roles for its fulfillment. Subjectivity also plays a part in an account of social relations—if not in 'role' directly, then in considering how the actor/thinker sees or assesses himself or herself as an eligible incumbent of a social role, that is, as a person involved in multiple relations and group membership and in which he or she participates and/or internalizes as a part of his or her identity.[19] The sources of roles and role behavior may be seen as entirely objective or subjective or, perhaps more commonly, as a combination of both. It is not always true that when both subjective and objective factors form a role it is readily recognized as a coherent, harmonious totality. Indeed, a given role may 'prescribe' conflicting and even obscure courses of action owing to differences of perspective. The 'prescription' that originates a role will likely determine its degree of structure, though roles may be changed or modified by actors while they are being played out.

THE INTERSUBJECTIVE APPROACH TO ROLE

As we have noted, the concept of social role brings a certain unified coherence to the formulation of a theory of coercion by facilitating a linkage between subjective and objective aspects of social behavior. Intersubjectivity in disclosing this connection blurs the formal distinctions between subjectivity and objectivity. Nothing in the analysis so far is meant to suggest that the concept of intersubjectivity as I have defined it will suddenly 'subjectivize' all objective terms or, contrariwise, objectivize all abstract, theoretical concepts. Instead, the intersubjective approach merely purports to show the ultimate reasonableness of 'mixed' definitions over those that ignore unavoidable and significant subjective aspects of social phenomena.

In this vein the concept of intersubjectivity becomes integral to the formulation of a role-based theory of coercion. The participants who are involved in a social action and reciprocal exercise of control are understood by one another as capable of bestowing and receiving meaning. Specific, situation-based meanings reflected in relational behaviors are mutually comprehensible by virtue of intersubjectivity. It is my claim that intersubjectivity is a valuable approach to 'social role' as the essence of a typically overlooked aspect of many social relations. Further, it is a key concept in comprehending the connection between the objective and subjective aspects of coercion.

THE SOCIAL NATURE OF PERSONHOOD

We have already discussed 'personhood' as a *social* designation. We may understand personhood in this way because our identities as persons originate mainly in social conditions and relations. Nevertheless this approach does not assume a metaphysical priority of the claims of society over those of the individual. Instead, it refers to the essence of humanity as rooted in its biogenetic and social relations. The social context of our upbringing and biogenetic heritage assures that we acquire our capacity to live and function as persons in society from a variety of sources. Among such sources we can identify genetic, ethnic, linguistic, and other cultural and intellectual influences that shape what and who we are as persons.

The most fundamental insight of our intersubjective awareness is its continual revelation of the intrinsically social character of our daily existence and of the life center each of us is for the other. We see ourselves on one hand as *individuals* with our own distinctive attributes, yet on the other hand we view ourselves as members of society and social groups where we are engaged in a multiplicity of social relations by virtue of which we possess a shared set of features with 'similar others'. As we define our place in the context of our life circumstances, social roles form a large part of our self-definition.

However, the particular network or complex of social relations and roles that form the dominant, social side of our being is not simply related to us externally as the items in our house stand in connection to us. It is easily recognized that these 'external' relations are spatial relations, and although we may be able to alter some aspects of our relation to a specific item simply by changing places, we do not alter the externality of the relation by our movement. While most social relations have external features, they are not spatial.

In a different sense, many role structures and social relations remain 'external' to their participants. Often this is possible because the actor can focus his attention on certain behavioristic aspects of the role without considering or being affected by the relational ones. In this regard some roles do not become 'lived' relationships in the full sense of the term. The participants may view themselves, for example, in relation to a depersonalized 'other', as bank depositor, commuter, taxpayer, or consumer, yet these remain examples of role relationships similar to ones in which we all participate to a greater or lesser extent. In other words, not all role relations carry obvious aspects of either intimacy or close involvement. But even in those that do, as with children in role relations to their parents, the role-players are not always fully aware of all the role aspects that may be operating. Thus self-consciousness of one's role involvements is not a necessary condition for the performance of role behaviors and so does not become an *essential* feature in our definition of coercion.

There are, however, a great many references we could list of social relations that are readily and influentially internalized. It is primarily the set of internalized relations and social roles that shape our social identities. As with genetic lineage, which is an 'internal' biological dimension, or as with place of birth, which is an 'internal' cultural dimension, there are categories of *potentially* internalized social relations that defy empirical description. The extent to which such potential categories may become internalized varies in accordance with many circumstantial factors. It remains nevertheless that some social relations and social roles are readily internalized by most individuals; other relations become less internalized, perhaps, in part because they satisfy a lesser need and accordingly convey a less intricate network of power and control. However, the extent to which role relations become internalized is directly proportional to the influences they bear on the personal identity formation of the individual.

Finally, the process of internalizing certain role relations makes of us more than discrete members aggregatively related to or constitutive of society. For in our appropriation of language, culture, ethnicity, or family structure, in our ways of doing, thinking about, and valuing aspects of our lives, we become members of families, groups, and communities and so assume corresponding roles (and typically relate to others and identify ourselves in terms of these memberships). In general, we 'embody' the social totality through 'internal' relations, and we understand and, in turn, as individual persons, become constituted by the social totality.[20]

ROLE AND COERCION

The distinction between internal and external aspects of social relations may be helpful in understanding the phenomenon of coercion. When actions and social relations are subjectively defined, they receive their meaning from the participants' understanding, purpose, and so on. However, relations and actions also become meaningful in light of the role each participant assumes with respect to other participants. Our intersubjective world discloses before us other beings like ourselves, that is, 'lived centers of experience and action', whose plans may or may not include the objects of our own experiences. Actors may thus become players in the subjective roles others have cast for them. If the actor-participants in potentially coercive situations view themselves and each other in terms of a certain 'prescribed' role relationship, the connection between these individuals is established and maintained on the basis of internalized relations, despite external appearances. To conceive of these participants as if they were related externally by observable actions alone is a misconstrual of the nature of their relationship.

The face-to-face character of the encounters frequently found in coercive contexts facilitates an immediate awareness of the 'other' as a visible and tangible self-determined source of meaningful actions. It is the direct nature of this confrontation that allows us to interpret the overt, specified actions of the "visible other" in an intersubjective manner. We then learn to extend these experiences and their interpretations by analogy to situations where confrontations may be less direct. The other's intentions and meaning as manifested in his or her patterned behavior and sources of action form the overall framework for determining the presence, degree, and limits of coercion. In addition, the intersubjective view makes it possible to conceive rationally a person's 'will', 'intentions', 'motives', and the like as being on a continuum with his or her actions and purposes in view of his or her interactive role relations with others.

In an earlier chapter a definition of coercion was approached by means of an examination of such empirically derived categories as the coercer, P, the coercee, Q, and their related actions. The present chapter has been devoted to an exploration of nonobjective factors that are integral to the phenomenon of coercion, proposing that the concept of social role offers the most comprehensible framework for such considerations. In review, such nonobjective or abstract terms as 'will', 'consent', 'intention', 'motive', 'need', 'choice', and 'expectation' are as crucial to an understanding of coercion as are objectifiable, theoretical terms like 'agents' and 'actions'. I hold it to be a requirement for a scientific social theory to properly represent the human individual and the subjective features of social reality, social relations, and knowledge. While not properly an elemental category, *role* joins the more objective type of classification as an essential feature in our definition of coercion, for it is through the concept of role that coercion can be viewed as a dynamic social relationship of power and control.

The inclusion of subjective aspects of social existence into an analysis of coercion has been repeatedly defended here. I acknowledge that there may be many instances of coercion that can be readily identifiable as such primarily on the basis of objective considerations, for example, where P clearly compels Q to do something Q vocally resists doing. On closer analysis, disagreements frequently arise as to the coercive status of the event in question. In these instances, for a truer representation of the situational contexts of coercion, it may be necessary to know something of the background relationship between P and Q, including role changes that can occur throughout the coercive process. Having such prior knowledge of the subjective and intersubjective states of the participants does not objectify the abstract features identified above. Rather it permits the scientific observer to account for the meaning he or she brings to the social context under scrutiny as well as for the private meanings and purposes of the participants themselves. A definition of coercion must be sufficiently comprehensive to account for all relevant subjective considerations. What allows the inclusion of the 'subjective' in a scientific account does not amount to a begrudging accession by the scientific observer to objectively unfathomable data but rather a deeper grasp of the underlying intersubjective nature of all social reality and knowledge.[21]

The nonobjective terms contained in definitions of coercion are intersubjectively understandable in a way that is inaccessible through a purely objectivist approach. As subjective beings we are aware of ourselves and of our existence in an intersubjective world. However, intersubjective awareness at this level is not the same as knowledge and understanding of others in the world of social interaction. Intersubjective experience is the basic type of experience that happens between ourselves and other human selves. At the level of common sense or everyday social experience, we subjectively understand that our co-present human individuals are beings capable of social action; and that they do not merely make overt, physical (observable) movements. In other words, our fellow creatures are understood by us to have intentions, motives, expectations, and other subjective or personal mind events behind their overt actions. In this sense external behavior is typically experienced intersubjectively, as an outer manifestation of inner lives. Further, we comprehend that external behaviors are not always direct, uniform representations of internal states; e.g., an 'outer' smile and handshake may be an extension of friendship or, alternatively, an effort to cloak an inner contempt. It is a basic error to reduce the inner to the outer realm or to assume a one-to-one correspondence between them by judging the mental solely on the basis of the behavioral.

Thus our common and frequent openness and directedness towards others lie at the heart of concrete and intersubjective experiences and are manifestations of the role relationships that we form. What remains to be analyzed at this stage is the conceptual and perceptual impact that the concept of intersubjectivity may impart to each of the nonobjective criteria we have isolated. One does well to remember that the usage of these 'nonobjective' criteria has often been a disguised attempt to categorize a subjective reality as overt behavior or to reconcile what are actually aspects of dynamic role relationships to a static operational format. In my opinion these abstract categories are best understood through the contribution of intersubjective awareness and the role contexts in which these phenomena are expressed.

WILL AND INTERSUBJECTIVITY

Will has been provisionally defined in this chapter as an abstraction for someone's disposition, capacity, or power to make decisions and execute actions accordingly. At its most objective, and like all dispositional terms, it is an abstract term that refers to the degree of probability that certain sorts of behaviors will likely occur in a certain context under certain conditions. However, the sort of activity referred to by the term 'will' is a process that is largely mental or internal to the being whose disposition it is, and, as such, it is private and empirically unobservable. In essence, the conscious process of "willing" should be regarded as a subjective event with certain 'objective' correlates such as 'the object of willing', 'an act of willing', or 'what is willed'. It is important to note that the epistemological status of these correlates may or may not actually be objective. Hence, an 'act of will' may be as much a product of a personal degree of courage or of determination as of calculated or objectifiable behavior. The term 'will' is basically not comprehensible as viewed within an empirical framework.

It is erroneous to assume that the intersubjective approach denies all empirical judgments. It merely refers to the intrinsic awareness in each human being of similar and acting other beings. The knowledge of the existence of other beings occurs on the same precognitive level of awareness as the knowledge of what is experienced empirically through the senses. Thus, on this level, 'will' is not an abstraction but something understood as exhibited in another's actions, as it is observed in one's self. It is 'private' in the sense that each person has his or her own 'will', but it is not unobservable on that account on the intersubjective level, for it is in our actions (and inactions) that we perceive and 'understand' the will's activity. The 'subjective' does not lie behind the 'objective' but is essentially observable in the actions, interactions, and relations among people of which we are aware.

'Will' is an important aspect of the roles that play in coercion and can be regarded as an essential feature to a definition of coercion. These are our essential categories (ECs) introduced earlier as largely empirical.

Where P is the coercer, Q is the coercee, p is the instrumental action, and q is the coerced behavior.

$$P \longrightarrow p$$
$$Q \longrightarrow q$$

In real situations the prior possession of a will of P with respect to p and Q with respect to q is among the necessary prerequisites for coercion to occur. Among other necessary conditions, it is through a conscious abridgment of the willful actions of a participant that the roles among the above ECs are defined. Such abridgment cannot usually be determined merely by examining the actions (p, q) of either actor (P, Q) or of any combination thereof. It is not the activity but the willfulness that is the critical concept; and willfulness cannot be empirically quantified.

'Will' is represented as above in our schema of coercion; will is considered to be an attribute of an actor (P, Q) that becomes operationalized only with respect to a given action (p, q). 'Will' is guided by desire or intention. In some instances of coercion, when Q neither desires nor intends to do q but does q as a result of P's doing p, we say Q does q *against his or her will* because Q's will was insufficient to support his or her own desire or intention to resist doing q. Q's 'deficiency of will' in doing q is a contributing factor (together with other factors such as the coercion action or instrument, p) in Q's being coerced by P. 'P coerces Q' may indicate a type of coercion in which P compels Q to do something against Q's will. Q's capitulation to P may have been the result of Q's decision to mount resistance (unsuccessfully) or not to mount resistance (in recognition of P's superior power). In either case Q is presumed to have supplied the 'deficiency of will'.

If an actor (P, Q) could not even have willful intentions with respect to his or her own actions (p, q), then these actions could not be considered within the realm of coerced instruments or activities. For example, if q is a reflexive action such as eyeblinking or other uncontrollable phenomena, or if q is an impossible action for Q to perform, such as growing extra limbs (these being extreme examples), then q could not be in the realm of willful actions and hence not in the sphere for coerced activities.

A prior condition for an instance of coercion is that P knows and wills p and attempts to effect thus willed behavior over q, which is not an activity within P's repertoire of action. In this attempt, P knows that Q (and only Q) can *will* q but might not otherwise. Conversely, Q knows that P can *will* p or fears that P can *will* another undesired instrumentalized action (of coercion) that Q would wish to avoid.

Thus the subjective knowledge possessed by each actor about his or her respective will becomes translated into intersubjective knowledge during 'real-life' situations. In face-to-face encounters where actors experience each other as 'lived bodies' with like subjective attributes, they can make certain assumptions about each other's will, arising partly from personal assumptions made about their own will and partly from experiences with others. Accordingly, in attempting to expand the personal sphere of influence to q, P enters into a role relationship with Q even if the attempted coercive event is not successful. As our future discussion will show, the potential role relationships of P and Q as actualized in part through intersubjective awareness will influence the possible success of an act of coercion; but conversely, the role relationship will also be defined by the success or failure of such attempted acts of coercion.

CONSENT (PERMISSION) AND INTERSUBJECTIVITY

In the context of coercion the matter of consent involves only the coercee, Q, and Q's response to P's doing p or to P. It is a determination of willingness on Q's part and so is a particular act of will. Q may consent to something either explicitly or tacitly. If Q's consent is explicit, Q communicates his or her subjective affirmation in some public manner. Q's implicit consent is construed publicly on the basis of a 'moral equation' of sorts, for example, Q's behavior 'amounts to' agreement in cases where Q continues to enjoy doing/receiving something without visible signs of dissent. Even with such a strategy for objectifying 'consent', consent remains in both senses a subjective event, which may or may not be expressed publicly. 'Tacit consent' has been exemplified traditionally as someone continuing to live under a certain political regime reaping its benefits and shouldering its burdens and liabilities. This is a view of Jean Jacques Rousseau.[22] But this interpretation amounts to little more than asserting that consent is a more subtle form of objective, consenting behavior (i.e., no discernible evidence to the contrary is presumably sufficient evidence in support of 'consent'). Unless we are aware of Q's private judgments, values, and purposes, the meaning of the general tenor and series of involvements of Q's life to Q remains, for the observer, of incidental importance in a determination of consent. Though 'consent' (or dissent) may be the outcome of a cognitive process involving private mental discrimination and judgment, it may also occur instinctively and instantaneously, thereby distinguishing a noncognitive aspect of the term. In any case, 'consent' is always primarily a subjective term because as an internal event it requires among other things a certain act of will for its expression (even in its most subtle forms). Moreover, the objective definition of consent is further inadequate because there is no reliable empirical basis for distinguishing between implicit dissent and tacit consent or the action(s) of Q and the reason(s) behind Q's doing q.

An intersubjective approach is needed to comprehend the subjectivity involved in these distinctions and the objectifiable expressions of consent. In an important way intersubjectivity reminds us that a person is a being with an inviolable will of its own who has the subjective capacity for reaching and acting on decisions in the light of its own self-determined 'good'. (Philosophers generally consider the possession of these features as constituting 'moral independence' for the social beings possessing them.) It also reminds us that 'consent' may never be a purely subjective, self-determined outcome since many things from different sources may influence the formation of consent: from entirely subjective preferences and values to 'public' values, social roles, and powerful persons or groups (who may pose a threat or who are perceived as such).

The difference intersubjectivity makes in our grasp of consent is that now it can be understood as being not merely identical with 'consenting' behaviors (like verbal assurances or utterances), but rather that as persons our behaviors are accountable on the basis of external stimuli as well as subjective meanings that may or may not culminate in direct objective (communicative) expression. Though it may be useful and even necessary in some cases to reconstruct for specific purposes the likely set of subjective influences upon behavior solely on the grounds of the participant's behavior, the intersubjective approach allows us to rationally acknowledge that behavior is a response to different sorts of influences, subjective and objective. Accordingly, our knowledge of whether Q gives consent to (do) something—or our knowledge of what consent means in general—is based on our intersubjective awareness of the significance Q's action(s) has both for participant(s) and observer(s).

Q has been coerced by P if and to the extent that P forces Q to do q when Q withholds or refuses consent or gives consent solely because Q was constrained by P to do so. Conversely, coercion has been eliminated or mitigated in the relationship between P and Q only if and to the degree that the recipient of force, Q, consents to (or does not dissent from) doing q—at the time P's act of force, p, is applied. Besides the presence, absence, or conditions of consent, other factors are also necessary prerequisites to coercion, namely, the role relationship between P and Q and choice.

As a rule, 'consent' is, it seems, an essential feature in virtually all types of coercion, but there are some extreme exceptions. For instance, 'consent' may be set aside in a determination of coercion where Q's age is well below the legal limit of maturity: no matter how willingly Q does q in response to the demand by P, Q's judgment and action are not regarded (socially, legally) as wholly self-determined and responsible. Thus, the (legal, social) role relation between P and Q constitutes, in such cases, an important factor in coercion.

Our schema for 'consent' is as follows:

Where P is the coercer, Q is the coercee, p is the instrument of coercion, q is the target behavior for coercion, and C = q as an action that has (not) been consented to by Q in response to P or P's doing p.

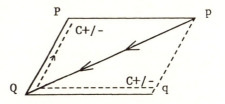

In coercion, although consent is subjective to Q, it is relevant only in Q's *relation* to P with respect to their actions, p, and q. Q's definite refusal to consent (i.e., in the form of active or passive resistance) is an essential feature of all clear-cut instances of coercion (physical and nonphysical). Moreover, it signals that once coercion has successfully occurred, Q no longer has control or, therefore, responsibility over his coerced action, q.

Consent (tacit or explicit) is also a necessary factor in the *degree* of coercion: it matters in regard to the conditions under which Q gives consent or how Q's consent is obtained. (For example, Q consents to q only because of disvaluable consequences caused by P for Q's noncompliance). Q's consent—although constrained by P or given reluctantly, makes Q partly responsible for doing q.

The intersubjective knowledge behind these considerations is that Q's social behavior is either self-willed/self-determined or, to some degree because of P, it is not. As our role example above indicates by implication, Q's wholly informal consenting to do q with regard to P is ordinarily an essential though not sufficient feature for determining noncoercive social relations, nor is its absence a sufficient feature for coercive relations by P and Q. Thus, consent is best understood as a nonobjective term whose place in a coercive event varies with the conditions and relationships (e.g., social roles) between the ECs as established by our intersubjective understanding.

CHOICE AND INTERSUBJECTIVITY

'Choice' may refer to the capacity to make choices or to 'having a choice', meaning the alternative opportunities open to a person. Like 'will' and other dispositional terms, 'choice' is an abstraction referring usually to a set of 'reasonable' behavioral expectations and explanations for persons 'under a given set of circumstances'. This empirical definition of choice ignores the fact that the act of 'choosing' or of 'making a choice' is mainly a mental-cognitive event. It refers to a voluntary mental act (or event) of selecting what the chooser prefers from a set of alternatives. To limit 'choice' to actions done or to courses of action operationally open to any person in certain circumstances is the result of an objectivist bias that is inadequate for comprehending the subjectivity involved in 'persons making choices' and 'some choices that persons make' (e.g., choosing to change one's attitude towards people, life, or tasks may or may not lead to determinate public or behavioral outcomes). In addition, it is fair to claim that 'choice' signifies a chooser's mind-state prior to (but causally linked with) the choice made, that is, that the chooser 'had a choice' refers sometimes as much to a subjective mind-state as it does to the range and objective status of certain choices. (For example, subjectively, a person has the capacity to offset his or her misdeeds and to choose a new course of action.) Therefore, a social theory utilizing 'choice' in its definition of coercion must not exclude its subjective dimension if it seeks to advance a more complete account of coercion.

In the earlier distinction drawn between 'action' and 'movement', we noted that the actor's 'having a choice' is exclusively an essential feature of 'action'. Since the relational view of coercion involves actions of participants as ECs, particularly the coerced action of the victim, 'having a choice' generally is an essential feature of a definition of coercion in all its various types. In a basic sense coercion is in part an interference with Q's choice-making capacity (e.g., techniques like drugs for changing someone's 'will') or with his or her choice or range of choices that in turn will influence Q's behavior.

In some instances coercion will indicate a focus upon only Q's *range* of choices, that is, P will close Q's hitherto available options except the one desired by P. In cases like this 'choice' becomes a more empirically verifiable term. However, its subjective correlate—which involves the mind-states or preferences of the subject-actor for whom the choice(s) has been largely predetermined by the coercer, P—is also an essential element in the relation. In the final analysis, choices become 'choices' for persons who prefer or choose them; they are not merely independent variables or isolated 'observables'. Further, the range and types of 'available' choices are often clearly fixed by the social roles assumed by actors.

The various stages of choice concern a 'capacity to make choices', 'having choices', and 'the means and opportunity to execute the choices made'. The latter involves the person's 'will', for without it, to carry preferences into effect, ultimately no human existence is possible. Hence, the following schema for 'choice' in our analysis of coercion includes the 'will':

Where P is the coercer, Q is the coercee, p is the instrumental action, and $q^1 \ldots q^n$ indicates there is a choice for P or Q within the repertoire of willful action.

P

($\pm$ will)

p
p^2
p^3

Q

($\pm$ will)

q
q^2
q^3

As the act of coercion takes place and Q exercises the coerced (or minimal) choice P constrains Q to make and act upon, the schema representing this dynamic event will look like this:

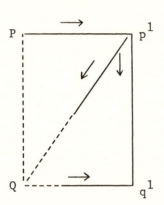

"_____" is the control P, Q has over doing p, q respectively; "_ _ _ _ _____" is the degree of control a participant has over his or her own action.

Here, Q retains some, though minimal, choice over doing q^1. For instance, Q may choose to resist—unsuccessfully—doing q^1. Indeed, the choice P constrains Q to make may be more subjective than objective, for example, when Q does q^1 because P has closed all other objective courses of action. But, in the end, P has greater control—in a successful act of coercion—over Q's doing q^1; and so, in a sense, q^1 (the final coerced 'choice' Q makes) is more (but not entirely) an action of P's than of Q's. Now, if Q *loses total control* over his or her doing q^1, it is no longer a coerced action of Q's, and Q becomes an instrument of P. On the other hand, if Q *has full control* over his choice, q^1, then P has failed to coercively control Q's action.

Sometimes the coercee is coerced because, it is claimed, that he or she 'had no choice' but to satisfy the demand of the coercer. As a nonobjective term in some otherwise empirical definitions of coercion as used in reference to the above instances, rendering 'choice' intelligible boils down to the most operationally effective strategy enabling the collection of objective evidence to demonstrate the likelihood of the victims having no (subjective) choice. The usual strategy consists in the adoption of the 'rational actor' model whereby it would-be calculated in terms of how a rational person might be expected to respond given a set of objectifiable conditions and approximately what the coercee's state of mind or choice-making capacity is at the moment of victimization. In any case, 'persons' are implicitly acknowledged by such strategists as subjective beings.

The intersubjective approach to 'choice', which the schemata are intended to represent, does not seek to circumvent its subjective status by regarding it solely in terms of what the 'observables' tell us about its presence. Instead it recognizes that 'observables' should be the focus for certain limited practical purposes, but, as to the subjective event of (persons) 'making choices', this goes to the heart of what we understand and experience as we experience ourselves and others like us intersubjectively and as persons.[23]

Therefore, without a basic intersubjective notion of *human* possibilities of choice-making, the full range of real (and not merely logical/empirical) alternatives can never be truly comprehended. And so coercion, if defined in the terminology of the objectivist (including the use of 'choice' as meaning objective possibilities), could be applied to an instance—as likely as not—of Q's feigning resistance to P's coercive action. Unless there were objective grounds for revealing the pretension of the 'victim', this would be classified as coercion when the subjective facts may be that for Q's own private purpose, the action was highly valued by him with or without the coercer's *apparent* influence. In sum, with intersubjectivity, we may not know any better whether Q's choice was a genuine one, but at least we have a basis for a unified social theory that can comprehend the possibilities.

INTENTION, MOTIVE, AND INTERSUBJECTIVITY

Very few definitions of coercion have any reference to 'intentions' or 'motives' as key terms. Those that do mean by these abstractions nothing more than certain subjective cognitive states of persons that are internal inducements to action. In their most empirical manifestation, a combination of factors work together to establish for the observer the possession of a specific motive or intention, inasmuch as this is never objectively self-evident. For the observer, the observation process objectifies the action being observed, thereby giving it the same status as what the external movements and other environmental 'observables' indicate the actor's goal is in doing what he does. Earlier we defined these terms as follows: a 'motive' is an internal cause of, or 'reason for', a person's mobilization of will and direction-force for the action done; an 'intention' is an object of thought, particularly something to be achieved by the person, or perhaps coupled with the 'will', to accomplish the motive. Nothing in an empirical survey of external realities alone tells the observer immediately and unequivocally about the specific motives or intentions of an actor. These are basically subjective events, beyond the reach of pure observation, and whose existence may not correlate directly with observed behavior.

The intersubjective approach does not interpretively 'construct' intentions and motives in the same way the empirical understanding does: by viewing them as hypothetical states whose sole significance is its objective aspect. Intersubjectively, it is the more basic inter-subjective knowledge of our human existence that actually rationa-lizes the objectivist's quest for intentions or motives and also allows for claims about them as important subjective realities that influence and explain behavior. Insofar as we are self-conscious, self-directing beings, the internal causes of behavior in general matter as much as external sources. Subjective states like intentions and motives are better treated from an intersubjective viewpoint that affords a more comprehensive, intelligible account of social behavior commensurate with our everyday experience of our own lives and of society.

In the terminology of some definitions of coercion already cited, the explicit appeal to motives and intentions is confounded because it has mistakenly presupposed that the actions of a participant will objectively show the causal link between, say, Q's doing q, because Q adopts the 'motive' for doing q that P wishes Q to have.

These definitions do not cover all types of coercion, but with respect to those that are covered, intentions and motives seem to be *variable* features necessary for only certain types of coercion. Apart from the few definitions containing them, intentions and motives are never really a central aspect of a coercive relation and so should not be considered on par with the ECs or other essential features or conditions. Though they play some part in some instances of coercion, even an important part, they never acquire the importance of the willful actions expressing them. Intentions and motives as subjective states have a more immediate relationship to the 'will' (of a participant), which impels the action done, than to the movement itself. Thus, they are not directly blocked or frustrated in coercive events, only the willful actions that spring from them are.

Finally, intentions and motives are in the broadest sense just common characteristics for the occurrence of coercion as they are for all actions (coercive and noncoercive) in general. Since actions are construed as never being mere random body movements, our intersubjective insight shows that P has (among other things) some motive or intention in doing willful action, p (and in Q's doing q). Both p and q become intelligible *as actions* and can be given justification partly in light of the participant's motives and intentions.

The issue at hand is how best to schematize 'intention' and 'motive' within the schema introduced earlier when they do contribute to the formation of a coercive relation. The old format for 'will':

Where P is the coercer, Q is the coercee, p is the instrumental action, q is the target behavior for coercion, and (± will) indicates that p, q is in the (respective) class of willful actions of P, Q.

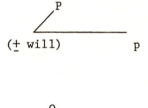

(± will)   p

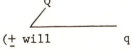

(± will   q

In role-structured social relations, which are of a coercive kind, the importance of intentions/motives can range on a sliding scale from being subjectively crucial to the performed actions(s) to being incidental, as when Q's (coerced) capitulation to p (of P) is the direct result of cowardice (a deficiency of will) rather than of Q's role-defined intention to do otherwise being thwarted. A role relationship may fix the role-player's intentions and/or motives while, on the other hand, the role player may establish a subsequent role relationship in terms of which P and Q interact. Further, they are part of what is essential to the subjective formation—and ultimate intelligibility—of the participant's willful actions *as actions*, which are expressive of coercive power relations particularly involving social roles. Objectively defined, tightly structured customary roles tend to yield highly predictable patterns of behavior in participants. For example, a central part of P's job description calls for P to do p to Q (which P always does) in order to get Q to do q. P's 'intention' to do p with respect to Q and Q's response to P are highly (but not invariably) predictable in this context. Despite this apparent objectification of P's and Q's subjective states, intentions and motives remain subjective states and are best seen as variable features that may acquire greater or lesser importance depending upon the kinds of roles by which the reciprocal relations and actual practices of participants are defined.

Intentions/motives can now be incorporated into our schema, as it is supposed to depict these nonobjective terms in connection with ECs of coercion:

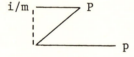

Where P is the coercer, Q is the coercee, p is the instrumental action, q is the target behavior for coercion, and i/m indicates there is an intention/motive for P or Q which may/may not be executed.

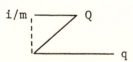

In deliberate acts of both physical and nonphysical coercion where P intends or is motivated (by interest, desire, belief, value, and so on) to coerce Q, i/m is essentially a cognitive subjective state that becomes important in P's forming p. For Q, on the other hand, an i/m may not even be of secondary importance in Q's coerced response (e.g., where Q's capitulation may be the result not of any intention of Q's but because Q lacks the will to resist). In any case, it is supposed that a specific i/m is more objectifiable in clear-cut instances of physical coercion owing to the obvious nature of the interaction between P and Q. But this supposition too easily overlooks that the nature and ultimately subjective cognitive character of an i/m means that somehow in the discernible interaction, to establish the coerciveness of the relationship, an observer must determine whether an i/m is present (at least in P's case) and to what extent it has influenced the (inter)actions of P and Q. This process is necessarily one of interpretation and never of immediate knowledge for the outside observer. (For instance, Q's coerced response may be the direct result of what P does, of what Q thinks P intends, or of the role relationship Q perceives between P and Q. It is not their remoteness from p and q in the chain of causation but their subjective nature that renders them matters of interpretive knowledge.) The presence or absence of an i/m contributes, always in tandem with other factors, to the success or failure of attempted coercion, as well as to the degree of coercion. In itself, an i/m always remains at best a secondary though necessary factor in an account of coercion. Even in an observation of actions, though reference to i/m in describing them sometimes seems unavoidable, an i/m is not as obviously manifest as the movement itself (or even the objective aspects of the role) is.

WANTS (w), NEEDS (n), WISHES (h), DESIRES (d), AND INTERSUBJECTIVITY

These terms are so much a part of our everyday vocabulary that we may forget that each is an abstraction refering to a large and not always distinct variety of human and individual capacities and functions. For instance, some 'n' are purely biological (procreation, nutrition), others are biosocial (the forms of sexuality and nutrition production or acquisition), and still others may be wholly psychological (self-mastery), and so on. Depending upon what we are talking about, 'need' may mean various things and so, accordingly, may require different definitions. Further, some may be in the nature of background influences on behavior generally, whereas others may be particularly 'pressing' and 'unavoidable'. To make broad and useful generalizations about these abstractions taken together, it is necessary to recognize that none of these are empirically observable in themselves nor are they always correspondent with or reducible to observable body states and activities. In fact, 'd', 'w', and 'h' are internal mental phenomena that are qualitatively different from any neuroelectrical conditions that may determine and correspond to them. (Therefore, it is my view that even if ways are found eventually to correlate brain activity with the specific actions of an animal, it may be established that animals are capable of cognitive consciousness, but it will not be established that an animal is nothing but a network of neuroelectrical impulses.) (Thus, when we say Martin Luther King 'had a dream', we do not mean only that he had neuroelectrical patterns in his brain). The class of n or n-functions may seem at times to be the most definitive of our essence as human persons, more so perhaps than the others (w, h, d) and, hence, the most 'objective', but they are not more objective, simply because they are universal, basic, and necessary to our existence.

From the point of view of objective human behavior we assume a causal connection between certain behaviors and 'n, w, h, and d', that is, we use these terms to explain such behaviors (e.g., X eats to satisfy his or her nutritive needs). Hence, the terms are essentially unobservable capacities and events of the inner integral life of every person, which may or may not be satisfied, acted upon, or expressed beyond one's subjective or internal existence.

That persons have such things as n, w, h, and d is self-evident both in our own and in others' behavior, (i.e., for us to certify their existence in general requires no proof or additional evidence beyond perceptible behavior) only because we have an intersubjective awareness of ourselves and 'others like us' as persons. This means, in part, that we see each other and ourselves as living beings whose essential, vital, internal features include these things and whose behavior expresses them. This perspective is acquired not from observation of behavior alone but from intersubjectivity.

Very few definitions of coercion actually use these nonobjective terms, but in those that do, certain constraints are placed on their possible meanings owing to the context (of coercion) in which they are to be understood. Coercion involves an interactive relation between at least two participants where one controls either the person or the behavior of the other; imposing some determinate interference upon the behavior of the other and to that extent controlling the other's behavior may be accomplished by controlling the coercee's action, body, or environment. As applied to n/w/h/d, the behavior must be an expression of one or more of these, that is, a furtherance or satisfaction of them. Consequently, 'coercive control' refers to an unwelcome interference by another in the attempted movement from important n/w/h/d or internal mind/body states that urge and guide persons towards satisfaction.

In a less complicated sense another meaning that seems to describe the function of these nonobjective terms in a definition of coercion is to regard them as synonymous with 'will'—namely, 'against one's wishes' = 'against one's will'—so that what we have already said about the subjectivity of will and its shortcomings as used in objective definitions and about its ultimate comprehensibility from an intersubjective viewpoint applies equally well in their case.

These terms may be introduced into our schema without denying or falsifying their nonobjective status. Let n/w/h/d be symbolic representations of the essentially internal subjective features, capacities, and events of the inner lives of P, and Q with the understanding that any of these may be externalized, and hence objectified, in the form of expressive behavior.

Where p is the coercer, Q is the coercee, P is the instrumental action, q is the target behavior for coercion, and n/w/h/d indicates there is a need, want, wish, or desire for participants P, Q within the class of willful action, q is the target behavior necessary qualification in that although P's n/w/h/d may define P's role and explain his or her behavior, it is mainly Q's n/w/h/d that is central to the coerciveness of P when n/w/h/d are essential to the definition of coercion).

(I)

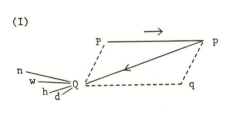

In Schema I, P is depicted as directly and coercively controlling Q and, in turn, indirectly controlling Q's action, q, by altering or extinguishing certain capacities Q possesses (e.g., Q's 'humanity' may be modified by drugs or brainwashing techniques or by torture and so on, which P forcibly imposes on Q's body, so that Q no longer does what P does not want Q to do).

In Schema II, which follows, coercion occurs as P 'coercively' interferes (not all interferences are coercive: some forms of paternalism increase rather than diminish the recipient's autonomy; only those opposed or resisted by Q are coercive) with the *action* Q takes as expressive of his or her (Q's) n/w/h/d. Our action may be taken in fulfillment of some basic urgent need, but 'will' may or may not play a fundamental role in this process, that is, we sometimes do things because of our need to do them, not because we desire or wish or even 'will' them; indeed, the 'will' may be powerless to halt certain movement brought on by 'need'. But perhaps there is a fine line (if not altogether indistinct) between purposeful action and action/movement inspired by 'animal necessity'. (By this I refer to the traditional and popular scientific belief that an animal behaves merely as a result of reflexes or of instincts that are determined by the genetic program in its central nervous system. This belief denies that animals think or 'have awareness'. Deciding the line of demarcation will ultimately resolve a question about whether interference in the behavior of other [nonhuman] life-forms like dogs, and so on can conceivably be coercive [i.e., preventing a hungry dog from getting at his food is both cruel and insensitive, but is it a form of coercion?]), thus, P interferes directly with q's being done and only indirectly with the n/w/h/d that causes and explains Q's behavior.

Again, I purposely omit reference to P's n/w/h/d because any role they play in 'coercion' is at best incidental (though it may explain and condition the role relationship between P and Q): they may show P's premeditation; promote the likelihood of P's being successful; or establish justification for coercion. But it is only the focus on Q and Q's relationship with P that is crucial for coercion because what counts is P's (coercively) controlling Q's behavior (and not what P's n/w/h/d might be in that regard).

(II)

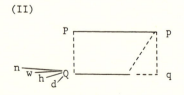

Neither Schema I nor II convincingly establishes that the features n/w/h/d of P and Q are necessary for all types of coercion. Together they exhaust all possible functions for n/w/h/d in coercion so at best we regard them as inessential variable features that may play no significant part in coercion but that, on the other hand, if they are not construed merely as synonyms of 'will' (in a definition of coercion), may identify some of the background features of Q compromised or seriously affected by some coercive actions.

These features are essential generally to Q's humanity but not necessarily to Q's being coerced. To take the most seemingly objectifiable of these abstractions, 'n', Q's basic social need to work for or produce a living, for example, may remain unmet because of something in particular P did or did not do. P's relationship with Q is never on this account alone coercive. What it does suggest is that 'Q's unmet n, due to P's (not) doing P', may be among the prior conditions that signal coercion has successfully occurred. Likewise, any of the other features may serve the same explanatory background function. The only defensible generalization here seems to be that the closer these features move towards being at the heart of Q's 'humanity' in particular actions and relations (e.g., in the exercise of will or rational capacity itself or in the making of life-plans, and so on), the nearer they are to being counted among the significant prior conditions of coercion. But most acts of coercion would not be any less coercive for not involving the victim's n/w/h/d.

Certainly it is the more usual case, when speaking of n/w/h/d from an objective viewpoint, to regard them as typically subjective or abstract phenomena, though perhaps correlatable at times with certain observable behaviors or behavior patterns. They are no less subjective and internal when seen intersubjectively. The overriding and sole advantage of the latter perspective is that the possibility of certain capacities like 'needs' would be incomprehensible if it was not for our most basic awareness of our being in the presence of similar subjective and vital beings. This explains why we implicitly recognize certain analogies as such. Mechanical-functional analogies such as a car's need for fuel or that certain conditions are needed for a temperature inversion, are implicitly recognized (despite pretensions by philosophical monists to the contrary) as *analogous* to human needs for nutrition, shelter, and so on. It is the connection we intersubjectively make between the latter and their essential relationship to human vitality or life that renders such comparisons as being 'analogous'. Neither cars nor temperature inversions have literal 'needs' as humans (and other life-forms) do. It is more challenging to distinguish sophisticated robots from entities having 'human vitality' (e.g., having feelings and thoughts), but unless we recognize that this distinction is made on a deeper level of awareness than cognition (viz., intersubjective), very little on the various levels of cognitive consciousness could persuade us otherwise (i.e., that robots are simplified persons, or persons are complex robots).

Some n/w/h/d may shape a relationship between two parties, or they may be engendered by a certain preexisting role relationship. For example, in Schema I, a profound need for companionship may bring two parties together; in Schema II, a need may be felt by each member to keep the family to which they belong united. In such cases, n/w/h/d become important contributing factors in defining the relationship and interaction between P and Q. Accordingly, they are best understood as intersubjective aspects of coercion because it is in the mutual awareness of one's role (and n/w/h/d) with respect to the 'significant other' that the participant's interactions are to be understood.

Expectation (T): An 'expectation', as described earlier, is an inner, subjective, mental event, and as such, to the outside observer, it has a nonobjective status (though objectivists generally reject substantive ontological claims for subjectivity, including the thesis of causal efficacy where subjective mental events cause behavioral responses). It is a truism that people very often determine their behavior in the light of their 'expectations'. Accordingly, in the context of coercion, Q may yield to P's coercive demand due simply to the anticipation of a costly penalty by P in response to Q's noncompliance. The inclusion of 'expectation' in a definition of coercion is reasonable, provided, in part, that its nonobjective nature is not misrepresented or misplaced in its description following an objective interpretation. For by doing so the definition loses some of its objectivist force unless, in accord with a general theory of empiricism, it considers the notion as satisfactorily explicable on whatever objective basis our experience offers for it.

On the other hand, it takes a broader view of experience to found the claims about the cognitive (human) capacity to make plans (i.e., to have foresight, expectations, or anticipations and an awareness of possible consequences from various actions, and so on) or about the subjective mental world in general. The intersubjective perspective reveals the deeper level of experience from which comes both our awareness of ourselves and 'others like me' as subjective beings sharing a common world and the interactions and influences that make our different forms of social knowledge possible. It allows us to make proper sense of the subjective mental phenomenon of 'expectancy' because, after all, it is a subjectively meaningful notion that is rooted in the life of our intersubjective consciousness. That is, we as conscious human persons are always oriented towards a future and have an abiding sense of duration and change that we undergo in reciprocal and mutual relation to other selves and things.

Q has at any given time a dynamic repertoire of expectations (T^1, $T^2 \ldots T^n$) regarding all kinds of things, but our present focus is restricted only to those involving P, P's anticipated action (with respect to Q), and P's relation to Q. In reality these three objects are not usually grasped by Q in isolation from each other, for example, P is actually inseparable from his or her action(s), though for analytical purposes it is good to make the distinction. However, as action q may (not) be a causal consequence of Q's T, only the q need concern us because this is the one(s) influencing Q's (coerced) behavior. Coercion is a behavioral social relationship. P cannot coerce Q into having a specific T because P never has control over Q's thoughts.[24]

Expectations are 'anticipated outcomes' and as such can affect real outcomes. Q may expect a certain (un)desirable outcome (T^1) as a result of (not) doing q, so other things being equal, Q decides not to do q in the light of T^1. In general, T influences in part the choices we have, the decisions we make, and the feelings we have, all of which influence our actions in turn. With respect to coercion, outcomes are construed in terms of the influence doing q, or not doing q, is calculated to have on P (meaning also P's likely response and P's relationship to Q). Therefore, since physical coercion is a type that precludes any role for Q's $T^1 \ldots T^n$ (because Q's particular state of mind is irrelevant to the coerciveness of p), T is a variable only with respect to nonphysical types of coercion. In the latter, the eventual success or failure of attempted coercion may depend primarily on Q's (set of) T with regard to P. For the coercer, T as a subjective mental state is relevant in an analysis of coercion only insofar as it influences P to attempt to coerce Q; otherwise, it is irrelevant. For the coercee, on the other hand, T plays some part in the final success or failure of P's attempted coercion and in determining a social role relationship between P and Q as well as Q's actions and P's response to Q.

In general, then, T functions in coercion as a variable feature that may be important for some nonphysical types of coercion. But since T is never empirically observable, to understand the part it plays in a definition of coercion requires an intersubjective approach to the primary ECs. The intersubjective perspective does not reveal special knowledge of, or make visible to the objectivist's observation, subjective mental realities otherwise closed to inspection. Instead, it enlivens and deepens our view of 'experience' and fully respects our knowledge of ourselves and each other as subjective beings with an inner mental life partly describable in terms of 'expectations'—and hopes, fears, wishes, beliefs, biases, etc.—as we face or interact with, and generally relate to, others.

Our schema for 'expectation' as it occurs in some instances of 'nonphysical' coercion is as follows:

Where P is the coercer, Q is the coercee, p is the instrument of coercion, q is the target behavior for coercion, and T^n is the expectation or set of expectations that Q has that leads to Q's being coerced to do q.

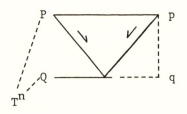

When T^n does lead to Q's doing coerced action q, both participants, P and Q, play some part in determining Q's behavior, as this schema represents. For example, it is Q's decision to yield to P or to P's threat (an expectation of costly harm), and it is P's threat (p) or the threat P himself poses to Q—along with Q's desire to avoid the consequences threatened by P or posed by P in and because of P's relationship to Q—which together contribute to Q's doing q. In general, T^n is a mental act and configuration of Q's that, by contrast to its place in coercion, may or may not induce Q's action, depending upon any number of relevant factors: the role relationship between the actors, Q's values, beliefs, perceptions, goals, interests, 'will to resist', and so on.

When T is a significant factor in some instances of (nonphysical) coercion, role relationships that may define or be defined in part by Q's T^n will affect Q's (coerced) behavior in relation to P. Suppose Q holds a certain position that places him in future dealings with P in a subordinate position. Objectively, it seems that P has more power over Q in terms of his role in the relationship than Q has over P. This ostensible 'fact' becomes the explanation of Q's (coerced) capitulation to P. A different account of the same situation arises intersubjectively, where Q may be aware that his or her role in the relationship with P places him or her—in his or her anticipation of future dealings with P—in a subordinate position. In other words, Q's awareness gives rise to a certain T^n reflecting that position. Objectively, Q's capitulation to P will be seen as a result of 'subordinate position' or of 'P's superior power'. Intersubjectively, Q responds to P in terms of the T^n Q has of P. This can be seen if Q does not capitulate to P's attempted coercion; P's failure to control (and to coerce) Q in this regard is the result not of objective relative position or power exercise, but of Q's T^n (e.g., Q expects P not to punish or else to punish so lightly as to sufficiently discourage capitulation). Of course, P may coerce Q because Q expects severe penalty, though Q's behavior will seem like noncoerced compliance if it were not for Q's T^n. In short, T is an intersubjective feature in coercion.

It is our intersubjective consciousness of T that modifies our view of the relationship between P and Q and reveals how T can play a part in their interaction.

SUMMARY

The foregoing discussion has been a preliminary exploration of a way in which certain subjective or pre-objective states that may be involved in coercion can best be comprehended through relational and intersubjective considerations. In the coercive context, while each participant may be considered as having a potential 'sphere' for action and responsibility, the nature of relational existence in concrete everyday life does not permit anyone a complete, unlimited sphere of self-control. Hence, in light of our analysis, it does not make sense to define coercion in terms of a denial of or absence of absolute self-control or of 'freedom to control one's actions' because in doing so one would imply that the 'coercee's' prior sphere was complete.

Role should rather be considered as a dynamic concept involving relations that may change over time. Such changes take place in accordance with a number of variables through which external relations become internalized. An elaboration of each of these variables may ultimately be reduced to considerations of freedom and autonomy and their reciprocal and limited ranges for each participant. In the next chapter we will explore the idea that it is in the reciprocal modifications of such spheres and their relative growth, diminutions, and overlappings that coercion takes place.

Persons are essentially social beings in possession of a certain range of social autonomy. In power relations, and especially with respect to coercion, the autonomy of a participant is not to be viewed as a pre-formed or static sphere carried into and throughout the relationship. Rather, the relation may be coercive in virtue of the coercer's having exercised power over the coercee diminishing the sphere of autonomy of the latter over his or her own person or action.[25] The leading idea behind social autonomy is that social relations influence the participants' relative and shifting spheres of autonomy.

NOTES

1. Virginia Held, "Coercion and Coercive Offers," in *Coercion: NOMOS XIV*, J. R. Pennock and J. W. Chapman, eds. (Chicago: Aldine-Atherton Press, 1972), pp. 50-51. Bernard Dauenhauer, "Politics and Coercion," *Philosophy Today* (July 1978), p. 109. Martin Gunderson, "Threats and Coercion," *Canadian Journal of Philosophy* 9, 2 (June 1979), p. 251. Mark Fowler, "Coercion and Practical Reason," *Social Theory and Practice*, 8, 3 (Fall 1982),pp. 333-34, 347, 350. Bernard Gert, "Coercion and Freedom," in *Coercion*, Pennock and Chapman, eds., p. 32; also, in this vein, where the coercee "could reasonably have done otherwise," see Gerald Dworkin, "Compulsion and Moral Concepts,"

Ethics 78, 3 (April 1968), p. 232; other terms like "choice," "intent," and "unwillingly" punctuate Dworkin's various descriptions. Patrick Wilson, "Ryan on Coercion," *Mind* 91 (April 1982), pp. 262, 263. Harry Frankfurt, "Coercion and Moral Responsibility," in *Essays on Freedom and Action,* Ted Honderich, ed. (London: Routledge and Kegan Paul, 1973), p. 66. Michael Taylor, *Community, Anarchy, and Liberty* (New York: Cambridge University Press, 1982), pp. 18-19.

2. For example, Held, "Coercion and Coercive Offers," p. 60.

3. H. J. McCloskey, "Coercion: Its Nature and Significance," *Southern Journal of Philosophy* (Fall 1980), pp. 343-44. In his critique of a view of some social contract theorists that 'consent' to a system of coercion, whether legal or political, McCloskey removes the possibility of the system's coerciveness. Hence, the just state is one instituted by 'consent of the governed' and so is at its institution, uncoercive.

4. Gunderson, "Threats and Coercion," p. 251.

5. Gert, "Coercion and Freedom," p. 34.

6. It was important enough to have drawn the attention of a number of systematic philosophers like Hume and Descartes. Hence, I disagree with the claim that intersubjectivity never emerges as a significant problem in traditional philosophy. See E. Mounier, *Existentialist Philosophies,* Eric Blow, tr. (New York: Macmillan, 1949), p. 72; also see Thomas Owens, *Phenomenology and Intersubjectivity* (The Hague: Martinus Nijhoff, 1970), p. 1.

7. *The Philosophical Works of Descartes,* vol. 1, E. S. Haldane and G.R.T. Ross, tr. (New York: Dover, 1931), pp. 219-27, 345-46, 350.

8. David Hume, *A Treatise of Human Nature,* L. A. Selby Bigge, ed. (Oxford: Oxford at the Clarendon Press, 1955), pp. 252, 253, 254.

9. Ralph Barton Perry, *Present Philosophical Tendencies* (New York: Greenwood Press, 1968), pp. 129ff, 133, 134.

10. The methodogenic problems resulting from the misapplication of a method is discussed by Marvin Farber, especially in the context of his naturalistic critique of phenomenological idealism and other types of philosophies of experience. See Marvin Farber, *Basic Issues in Philosophy: Experience, Reality, and Human Values* (New York: Harper, 1968), pp. 83-85.

11. In this, they follow the lead of the nineteenth century philosopher, J. S. Mill, in his effort to solve the problem through a combination of observation and inductive reasoning. See his *An Examination of Sir William Hamilton's Philosophy,* J. M. Robson, ed. (Toronto: University of Toronto Press, 1979), pp. 190-95, 204-5.

12. A. J. Ayer, "One's Knowledge of Other Minds," in *Essays in Philosophical Psychology,* R. F. Gustafson, ed. (Garden City, N. Y.:

Anchor Books, 1964), p. 364; Norman Malcolm, "Knowledge of Other Minds," in Gustafson, pp. 373-75.

13. See Alfred Schutz, *Collected Papers,* vol. 1, (The Hague: Martinus Nijhoff, 1967), p. 163; see Schutz's *Collected Papers,* Vol. 3 (The Hague: Martinus Nijhoff, 1966), p. 161ff.

14. M. S. Frings, "Husserl and Scheler: Two Views on Intersubjectivity," *Journal of the British Society for Phenomenology* 9, 3 (October 1978), pp. 147-49.

15. Maurice Natanson, *The Journeying Self* (Reading, Mass.: Addison-Wesley, 1970), p. 32.

16. For example, such 'truths' as the complexity and nonpassive character of conscious experience, the incompleteness of cognitive knowledge, and the concept of intersubjectivity not merely as a product of experience but also as a formative contributor to experience.

17. In Max Scheler's words, "the *essential* character of human consciousness is such that the community is in some sense implicit in every individual." Max Scheler, *The Nature of Sympathy,* Peter Heath, tr. (Hamden, Conn.: Archon Books, 1970), pp. 218, 219-30; one can only wonder about which 'community' Scheler has in mind.

18. R. S. Downie, *Roles and Values: An Introduction to Social Ethics* (London: Methuen and Co., 1971), p. 128; Dorothy Emmet, *Rules, Roles, and Relations* (Boston: Beacon Press, 1966), p. 15; and Norman Bowie, *Business Ethics* (Englewood Cliffs, N. J.: Prentice-Hall, 1982), pp. 2-4.

19. Alfred Schutz, *Collected Papers*, vol. 2 (The Hague, Netherlands: Martinus Nijhoff, 1964), p. 272.

20. Although it is not always perfectly clear whether one or the other, our individual relations to collectives such as various groups or organizations or even society *writ large* may be internal or external. For example, see Richard T. DeGeorge, "Social Reality and Social Relations," *Review of Metaphysics* 37 (September 1983), pp. 5-7, 9.

21. An effort to locate both subjective and objective theoretical terms within a single unified scientific theory of society and human behavior without disparaging one side of the dichotomy in favor of the other—e.g., using the concept of 'reason-explanation' as a type of cause of behavior; defending an interpretative understanding of social life, but from a 'scientific realist's' point of view—is found in Russell Keat and John Urry, *Social Theory as Science,* 2d edition (Boston: Routledge & Kegan Paul, 1982), pp. 27-45, 151-59, 167-75; also, for an intriguing discussion of the 'grounds of reason' from a perspective opposed to 'conceptual analysis', see Stanley Rosen, *The Limits of Analysis* (New Haven: Yale University Press, 1985), pp. 216-60.

22. Jean Jacques Rousseau, *The Social Contract and Discourse on the*

Origin of Equality, L. Crocker, ed. (New York: Washington Square Press, 1967), pp. 32-36.

23. I am addressing primarily the choice-making capacity and the subjective freedom we experience as we make choices. I am not referring to the possibility alone of objective alternatives from amongst which one may choose. If this was my reference, then, in the context of coercion, 'having no choice' would mean either no possible course of action to choose or only a single possible course of action: the one the coercee takes. In both cases, knowledge of external circumstances (alternatives) would be sufficient in determining the possibility of choice. However, a participant may choose not to pursue the only available observable course or even choose 'not to choose', i.e., abdicate decision-making and let things happen as they will. With the latter, a survey of the empirical possibilities will yield nothing of this kind, for the best yield would be abstract *logical* possibilities and relationships. (E.g., the logical possibility of doing x, -x or y; or the logical relationship that signifies that if P does not do -x, P must have done x or y). But never do we reach a knowledge or even awareness, operationally, of the subjectivity of the chooser. We may note two recent attempts to treat the agent's goal-seeking activity as an objective process, but it is conceded that little progress has been made in expanding information-processing theories to include motivational and emotional mechanisms. See H. A. Simon, *Models of Discovery* (Dordrecht, Holland: D. Reidel, 1977); and James J. Albus, *Brains, Behavior and Robotics* (Peterborough, N. H.: BYTE Books, 1981), Chapter 5.

24. This is evident in the case of successful 'brainwashing' where Q's thoughts are not really Q's own because Q has lost his or her 'mental' autonomy almost entirely. Brainwashing techniques, or how they are plied, may originally coerce Q, but once brainwashing is accomplished, Q becomes more or less an instrumental action or an instrument of P, and thus has lost a sufficiently important measure of self-control or self-hood.

25. It is important that we do not confuse this notion of social autonomy with the concept of a primordial or essential autonomy as in the familiar thesis of the 'inalienability of moral autonomy' associated with the philosophies of Kant, Rousseau, Spinoza, and Locke. In accord with these views, the moral agent whose autonomy is held to be inalienable is the rational individual human person. Hence, it is claimed that all such persons are equal in their autonomous moral agency. By contrast, our concept of social autonomy does not function as a 'fixed point' in the formation of a moral contract for the just community, as in the case of moral autonomy. For example, see the discussion in Arthur Kuflick, ''The Inalienability of Autonomy,'' *Philosophy and Public Affairs* 13, 4 (Fall 1984), pp. 271, 275, 296-98.

CHAPTER 4

Autonomy and Coercion

In this study generally I regard autonomy as the main concept in understanding what coercion is. Although some analysts say that the concept of freedom is most important, while others claim that 'force' is crucial, I hold that autonomy is of central importance.

Many philosophical discussions of 'autonomy' and 'freedom' cite coercion as the classical form of opposition to, or forfeiture of, either/both autonomy and freedom. But as we examine how autonomy relates to coercion, it becomes clear that it is my concept of social autonomy that is crucial in determining the presence of coercion.

In the social meaning I intend here, autonomy refers to the range of control the participants in a particular social situation have with respect to each other over their own private actions and over the exercise of their respective processes of decision-making, valuing, and willing. Autonomy is thus a relational notion because the actual range of a participant's social autonomy is mostly a function of his 'role' relatedness to the other participant(s). Accordingly, as the relations between participants change, it is likely that a corresponding modification in their respective and reciprocal ranges of autonomy will occur also.

The presence of coercion means that a victim-participant has lost some prior degree of autonomy over himself in the situation because of the coercer-participant's exercise of control over the victim in that limited respect. Through an exercise of coercive control, the coercer's range of autonomy is now increased, extending over the coercee's previously held autonomous sphere and at the expense of the victim. As we shall see later in this chapter (and in the last chapter), once someone has lost some degree of autonomy to someone else, then, unless it is reclaimed, no further *coercive* control of the victim in that regard is possible, since he has no social autonomy to lose. Hence, the controllee becomes in this limited way a mere instrument of the controller as the controller continues to exercise control over the controllee. Without autonomy, there could be no coercion. The deep-rooted sense even a child feels for the integrity and vitality of his or her own social autonomy lends a concept of coercion its normative character. Sometimes a child may object to an adult's request, not because the request is unacceptable, but because the unwanted prospect of relinquishing some degree of autonomy and so becoming a mere instrument of the adult is so abominable.

There exist differences of opinion about how to understand the nature of the relationship between coercion and autonomy. Usually, they are conceived in terms of one another. For instance, coercion has been construed as an imposition by another person upon someone's (autonomous) will. Conversely, autonomy has been interpreted as signifying the absence of any control relationship where coercion is a type of relationship between two parties in which one controls the action(s) of another in certain ways.[1] The latter is a 'nonnormative' approach to the concept of autonomy and represents a departure from most previous treatments in which value-related concerns were central. Later in this chapter I intend to improve upon this nonnormative definition of autonomy by including aspects of it in my own more complete idea of autonomy and coercion.

Owing to a certain conception of human nature that can be considered an important legacy of the eighteenth-century philosopher Immanuel Kant (1724-1804), the concept of a rational, self-determined, free-willed (or 'autonomous') being has come to be seen as the supreme value. Accordingly, if coercion treats individual human beings as if they are not self-determining, free beings (e.g., by bending the victim's will to that of the coercer), it treats them as something less valuable than their 'essential' selves and, in short, destroys their human dignity.[2]

The concept of autonomy (and of freedom) is similar to those concepts we introduced in the last chapter because they are, or refer to, nonempirical phenomena (unlike the 'elemental category', EC); they may be framed in objective language as is evidenced in some treatments like the one noted above. Perhaps the most obvious explanation behind attempts to objectify these concepts originates in our cultural need to conceptually grasp and control social reality scientifically. The problem remains, however, with respect to nonempirical and/or subjective phenomena (and to 'theoretical' terms), to find the best or most fruitful model for understanding them from a scientific point of view.

In our allusion in the last chapter to the limitations of a strictly objectivist approach to the social world and to 'social' experience, we tried to show that intersubjective language and perspective will help in dealing with certain nonempirical concepts, among which we include social 'autonomy'. Yet, nonempirical aspects of human autonomy and freedom have not prevented philosophers and social scientists in recent years from treating these concepts (in their social meaning) objectively or framing them only in objectivist or 'operational' language.

Some additional background about 'autonomy' will be useful before we examine in some detail the nonnormative 'operational' approach to the concepts of coercion and autonomy referred to above.

The etymological derivation of 'autonomy' is from the Greek: *autos* (self) and *nomos* (rule, law). In Greek history a city-state had *autonomia* when its citizens were governed by laws of their own making rather than by "laws or force of a foreign or conquering power."[3] In current usage, as well as in a personal or moral sense, we speak of autonomy as similarly meaning 'independence' or 'self-rule'. Owing mainly to the Kantian influence, persons having reason and a free will are described by virtue of these possessions as being 'autonomous' beings. Our treatment of one another and ourselves in view of our 'autonomy' continues to be a matter of serious philosophical debate. For instance, is 'autonomy' the most important human value (springing from the absolute inviolability of the human person), or does it share its place among other supreme values? In either case, anybody or anything forfeiting or diminishing autonomy would be considered as constituting a *prima facie* offense against autonomy. The same reasoning generally holds for 'freedom' in the sense that, in our philosophical beliefs, curtailments of freedom are *prima facie* in need of justification. In the context of the following discussion, I shall distinguish between the concepts of social autonomy and social freedom. For now, given this tradition, the point we wish to make is that insofar as coercion is conceived to be a usurpation of one's self-governance or independence or freedom *as a human person,* it is considered to be a *prima facie* evil.

Nothing I have said so far establishes the objectivity of autonomy and freedom. I have merely suggested the ordinary understanding we have of these concepts. A moment's reflection on the ordinary usage, whereby autonomy and freedom can be enlarged or diminished as an outcome of a certain policy or action, reveals that they are better thought of as 'spatial' metaphors, that is, their usage shoud be rhetorical or figurative and not at all empirical or objective. Metaphorical language, however, is not necessarily any less significant than literal usage.

It is in view of this background that efforts are made to objectify autonomy and freedom or to specify what they mean in an objective frame of reference.

Before we present in some detail an outline of a classic attempt at a thoroughgoing 'objective' analysis of autonomy and freedom and their correlative, coercion, some preparatory observations should be offered.

There is voluminous literature on 'autonomy' and 'freedom' and much dispute about what they do or should mean. But there is some general agreement also at least with respect to the etymological definition of autonomy and its Kantian reformulation. 'Freedom', on the other hand, has received an even greater plethora of interpretations.[4] However, in view of the concept of coercion, some restrictions are to be imposed on what these terms mean. From this point, autonomy and freedom will be construed objectively in terms of their social significations only. Secondly, social autonomy and social freedom will be defined in relational terms involving more than one participant. Lastly, these concepts will be considered only in the context of 'power' relations concerning either the presence or absence of a 'control' relationship between at least two participants. The presumption that lies behind these delimitations is that the factual (i.e., public and objective) links exhibited in these social relations can be more firmly established for the purposes of social science and are sufficient for an account of the phenomena under study. This claim, as I will show, is mistaken: 'operationalizing' our language will not yield an adequate or complete account of coercion and autonomy.

In his book *The Dimensions of Freedom,* Felix Oppenheim presents a philosophical theory of social freedom. His main task is an operational explication of 'social freedom', of 'social autonomy', of 'social control' (on which concept the distinction between the first two, turns), and of 'power' and 'unfreedom' social relations.[5] Though his focus is on relationships in the political domain, his claims may be generalized to cover many nonpolitical power relations as well. All these relevant relations may include persons, groups, governments, and political as well as nonpolitical agents as participants who stand in some social relationship to each other. In addition, his analysis is intended to include not only interpersonal and face-to-face relations among persons in small groups such as family, neighbor, or passerby but especially political and legal relations among citizens and governments, or between governments, that is, within federated systems as well as in international affairs. The terms of these relations concern the agents (or actors) and their actions that are analyzed as initiation and response (i.e., causal) behavior between agents. Insofar as actors are human beings or groups of human beings, they are described by Oppenheim as having the capacity for 'action' or 'agency'. He defines actions in terms of choice. In short, for an action, x, of an agent, X, to be an 'action', at least one alternative must exist from among which X chooses x. However, whether choice preceded X's action is ultimately a matter of inference from X's behavior. The process of inference is as close as Oppenheim's 'objective' approach allows the inquirer to get to the subjectivity of 'choice' in the determination of an 'action'. We shall return to this point later in our overall assessment of this objective approach.

Let us begin with a common enough international arrangement of our own to illustrate on the political level (as well as on the interpersonal level): Oppenheim's distinction between social autonomy and freedom. Suppose country X sells nuclear technology to country Y but sets as an exclusive condition of sale that the technology be used solely for nonmilitary purposes, q. In the context of this arrangement, X legally constrains Y to do q and so officially controls Y in this regard. Although Y lacks autonomy with respect to X in doing q, Y retains the freedom (it always had) to choose whether to apply its newly acquired technology to military or nonmilitary advantage. That is, X merely provided Y with the opportunity—and not the social freedom—to use nuclear technology. In terms of its standing in this relation to X, country Y is free but not autonomous, since Y's behavior is officially controlled by X.

On the other hand, in following Oppenheim's distinction, autonomy and 'unfreedom' are sometimes compatible (despite that 'autonomy presupposes freedom', a postulate which becomes clearer in an elucidation of the conceptual relationship between 'social freedom' and 'unfreedom'). To illustrate this point we recall from 1981 a short-lived political tempest that arose between President Reagan and his Budget Director, David Stockman. It concerned some unflattering remarks made by Stockman about "Reaganomics" (Reagan's economic program.) In Oppenheim's language we may say the following about this affair. If Reagan has influence over Stockman's not speaking his mind about "Reaganomics," then Reagan controls Stockman in this respect. However, this control relationship does not prevent or make Stockman unfree to speak his mind—which he did. Only afterward did his credibility suffer for a time in Congress (which made him unfree to some extent with regard to Congress, not to Reagan); he did not lose his job, so Reagan did not (beforehand) make it punishable for Stockman to speak candidly. Nothing restrained nor prevented Stockman from doing what he did, nor was it punishable; nor did Reagan have influence over Stockman's not making damaging statements about "Reaganomics." Thus, indeed, Stockman was autonomous in speaking his mind. His freedom was not restricted, and Reagan had failed to control Stockman in this respect. If he had eventually dismissed him for his "indiscretion," Reagan would have made Stockman unfree to speak his mind by making it punishable for him to have done so despite his failure to prevent or control Stockman's behavior. In summary, then, in speaking his mind about "Reaganomics,' Stockman would be unfree and yet autonomous (i.e., not controlled by Reagan).

SOCIAL AUTONOMY

By autonomy, Oppenheim does not mean an agent's relationless and abstract existence nor does he mean a condition or thing of such existence. There is no conception of 'autonomy in general', at least not in the objective sense intended by Oppenheim, there are only specific autonomy relations that may hold between any two agents in certain freedom or unfreedom and power relationships. He defines *social* autonomy in the context of specific interactive relations. By "social control," Oppenheim refers to a type of interactive relation (and not an object or property of some kind). Social autonomy is the negation of a control relation between two agents, though the denial of a control relation between two agents, where one either influences or restrains/constrains the action of the other, does not signal the complete absence of all relations.[6] A social control relation is only one kind of interactive relation, yet a very important and common one. Oppenheim holds: to the degree that agent Y has no control over agent X's conduct, x, then, with respect to Y (but not necessarily in relation to some other agent Z), X is autonomous in doing x.[7] The control process refers to any social process by which one agent causes another to behave in a certain way[8] or by which one agent performs a determinate action that would affect another's conduct if certain specified conditions were realized. The latter instance refers to the broader notion of 'having control' because it includes, among other things, the various types of 'exercising control'. Therefore, autonomy is meant to cover the denial of the broader relationship.

A controlled action is bordered on one side by inaction or a yielding to the actions of others and on the other side by autonomous action. For instance, inflation and recession may cause some people to commit larceny, but these conditions did not control them with regard to stealing, since they are neither agents (in Oppenheim's sense) nor sufficient causes of action. The holder of autonomy whose actions are not controlled by anyone in particular but whose actions are nonetheless subject to some agent's power or are involved in some network of freedom relationships demonstrates the fuller meaning of Oppenheim's concept of social autonomy.

But 'social' autonomy as a relational term is distinguishable from both 'power' and 'social freedom'. 'Having power' is the ability to control someone else's actions or to limit the other's freedom in some way.[9] To better locate 'autonomy' in Oppenheim's conceptual scheme, an explication of the concepts of power, freedom, and control, and their interconnections, is required.

Autonomy, again, is not something intrinsically valuable, for it has hierarchical value in Oppenheim's scheme: it is a type of power relation over one's own actions with respect to others, and it may include both freedom and unfreedom (i.e., punishability and prevention) relations but never (by definition) control relations.

When at least two agents are spoken of as being mutually independent, they lack power over each other's actions. Thus, autonomy relations are bordered on one side by the power to control[10] and on the other by independence or the lack of a power relationship. Non-power relations between agents are purposely excluded from Oppenheim's analysis because his concern is restricted to the objective features of social relations.

If Y has no power over X's doing x, then, unlike autonomy relations, we do not know in this case of independence whether X does x (we would know whether 'X does x' in the case of autonomy); nor can we, in this case, refer to X's autonomy in doing x since all power relations (and not merely control relations) are absent.

SOCIAL POWER

'Having power' is understood in Oppenheim's system as a dispositional concept in regards to an agent's capacity to control or otherwise limit the freedom of action of another agent in some specific manner.[11] Since it refers to the ability to influence, restrain, or punish (as a form of unfreedom), a power relationship between two agents may be categorized as 'autonomous' when no control relations exist, but, nevertheless, each may be unfree with respect to the other in some way. Agent Y may make it punishable for X to do x so that X's being punished for doing x shows Y's failure to control X's doing x. In other words, according to Oppenheim, autonomy and unfreedom relations may coexist, whereas autonomy and control relations are incompatible.

SOCIAL CONTROL

'Control' relations include two main types: influence and restraint/constraint. As a subcategory of control, an 'influence' relation means a causal relation between an agent's action and another's (i.e., the controllee's) choice to do something: Y influences (or controls) X to do x to the degree that X chooses to do x as a result of Y's action, y. 'Influencing' takes varied forms, including persuasion or dissuasion, deterrence, and conditioning. ('Information' control, through the use of computer technology, is a form of influencing because it affects awareness and action by regulating the flow of data to the agent, i.e., it externally controls what the agent experiences.) Constraining or restraining may indicate instances of physical violence, manipulation of a controllee's milieu or body, legal restraint, or threat of severe deprivation.[12] The latter forms of control affect courses of action, whereas 'influence controls' affect the controllee's choice only. Oppenheim's technical definition of 'control': Y controls X's not doing x to the extent that Y influences X not to do x or restrains X from doing x; 'control' is also exercised (and not simply 'had', in the positive sense) when and to the degree that Y influences or constrains X to do x.

'Exercising control' is by definition always successful. Some agent performs some specific influence or restraint action that constitutes a sufficient condition for the controllee's response behavior. 'Having control', on the other hand, occurs or exists whether or not the controller performs some control action. For example, in a hostage situation, the captors may have strong influence over their captives, who will comply with the captor's wishes not to escape without intending or attempting to do otherwise. Or, perhaps a less graphic example, voters often have influence over their elected representatives without exercising it in some way: they would dissuade or deter him or her from voting for a given bill before the legislature in case he or she should intend to do so.[13] Only when X does action x, and Y could not control its happening, is X autonomous in doing x with respect to Y. However, if we do not know whether X does x, then we have no knowledge whether Y has or lacks control over X's doing x or if X is autonomous in doing x. However, Y can limit X's freedom to do x where X does x anyway, meaning that X is autonomous in doing x despite Y's making X unfree to do x. Therefore, in Oppenheim's scheme, control and autonomy are linked to unfreedom relations. But also, 'social freedom' relationships may coexist with 'control' relations and, thus, exist in the absence of social autonomy.

UNFREEDOM

'Unfreedom' freedom relations are defined as a subcategory of power; and as an important type of limitation on an agent's freedom, it can be shown that the opposite of 'unfreedom' is not 'social freedom' but rather 'not being unfree' (i.e., a type of restriction on freedom). This distinction is necessary to show that 'social freedom' is not a synonym of 'autonomy' since unfreedom may be compatible with autonomy. Neither does 'being free' mean 'autonomy' because there are instances of freedom (involving control relationships) that are incompatible with autonomy.

The following example illustrates that 'not being unfree'—and not social freedom—is the opposite of unfreedom. No American citizen is made unfree to pay income tax. The government (or its agents) neither prevents anyone from paying them nor makes it punishable to do so. However, each citizen is legally required to pay taxes, so each is, with regard to the government, not officially free to pay income taxes, yet neither are they unfree. They are simply 'not unfree' and not free. The citizen is not officially free to pay taxes simply because he or she is not made unfree. Therefore, we see that social freedom is not the opposite of unfreedom; it is, however, the opposite of *not being free* to pay such taxes with respect to the government.

Other instances of restricting an agent's freedom besides preventing or making it punishable for him to do something may be cited. In 'not being free' to do something, then, an agent is not necessarily being made unfree. In any case, the opposite of 'not being free' is social freedom, and in distinguishing between freedom and autonomy, 'freedom' may coexist with 'control' relations whereas autonomy cannot. Some agent may be controlled in some respect by another and still retain the freedom to do or to not do something in that regard.

SOCIAL FREEDOM

What is 'social freedom? Objectively construed by Oppenheim, it means a certain relation between agents with regards to the actions of each (and is conceptually tied to the other relations we have described: autonomy, power, control, and unfreedom). In

Oppenheim's language: with regards to agent Y, X is free to do x to the extent that X is not unfree (i.e., prevented from or having had it made punishable) to do x, nor is X unfree to abstain from x (i.e., being compelled to do x). If it is not the case that X is not free to do x, X is free to do x. (But again, if X is not unfree to do x, X is not necessarily free.) For instance, according to a First Amendment freedom, it is unconstitutional to pass or officially tolerate laws respecting the establishment of a religion. In this sense, American citizens are officially free to pursue a religion of their own choice or not. This means that they are free from being compelled by law to do one or the other; they are not prevented from doing one or the other; nor is it officially punishable to do one or the other or to refrain from doing one or the other. In short, 'social freedom' relations exist, provided that Y does none of the following: (1) prevent X from doing x; (2) make it necessary for X to do x; (3) make it punishable for X to do x or, (4) refrain from doing x.

Social freedom, unlike control relations, does not entail any assertion regarding X's actual behavior because it always implicitly refers to at least two objectively specifiable alternative kinds of action. In short, with regards to Y, X is free to do or to not do x. For example, American citizens are free to vote or abstain to the extent they are not unfree to do either. Agent X is free to do x when: (a) X does x (of his own initiation or under Y's influence and is not being punished); (b) X does not do x even though X can do so with impunity; and (c) X cannot do x but not because anyone (prevented or) made X unable to do x.[14]

On the other hand, autonomy or 'lacking control' and 'having control' does tell us whether an agent does or does not do something. When one agent, Q, is free to do something, q, with respect to another agent, P, this signifies, again, that there is at least one alternative, p (to q), such that, with respect to P, Q is free to do q or p. However, we do not know which alternative action Q will do. Now, if p and q include all possible alternatives open to Q with respect to P, then no power (i.e., control or unfreedom) relationship exists between the given pair of agents. Also, Q is socially independent from p—but not autonomous—in that we have no prior knowledge of whether Q will do p or q. In sum, Q has both freedom (to do q or p) and independence (P has no power over Q), but Q cannot have autonomy ascribed to him or her in his or her relation with P. Finally, where there exists mutual freedom and independence (with respect to both P and Q), neither can prevent, restrain/constrain, influence or punish the behavior of the other. Hence, 'lacking control' is a sufficient condition for autonomy, but 'lacking unfreedom' must be superadded to negate the power relation and institute independence.

The concept of coercion ties in with the concepts of autonomy and freedom in the objective scheme we have just painstakingly described, but, before we elaborate upon the connection, some general comments are warranted respecting other definitions of autonomy and freedom that may be considered 'objective' (such as Oppenheim's approach).

OTHER 'OBJECTIVE' DEFINITIONS

Some philosophers define autonomy and freedom in *nonrelational* terms centering on a single participant, whereas others like Oppenheim define them in *relational* or multiparticipant terms. In the single-participant terms, certain characteristics define the autonomy of the single participant, for example, possession of a will, reason, the capacity to choose/consent, the early 'natural rights' ascription, internal self-control, self-realization, and, of course, freedom. In addition, some of these views closely link autonomy (of a single participant) with freedom as if they were synonyms, others tend to separate the two concepts or to deny any linkage whatsoever (indeed, nonlinkage between autonomy and freedom may be a direct outcome of a particular *conception* of the single participant.[15]

In relational theories involving more than a single participant, we find autonomy defined in terms of various *types* of relations, and, further, its conceptual connection to freedom specified on the basis of types of relations. For instance, some theories distinguish between autonomy and freedom due to rights-based relations,[16] equality-based relations,[17] or, as in Oppenheim's case, control-based relations.

On the whole I believe it is fair to say that those who treat 'autonomy' and 'freedom' exclusively in abstract, nonrelational terms diminish the scientific objectivity of their analysis owing primarily to the exaggerated importance given to *non*social factors.

However, a social conception of these terms is no guarantee of objectivity; yet without 'social context' the outcome of analysis is foredoomed as impressionistic, partial, and unscientific. As I have claimed elsewhere, though, the 'social world' has its important subjective dimensions, and a complete science of society must be able to comprehend this reality.

COERCION

How is 'coercion' connected with 'autonomy' and 'freedom' in the 'objective' or operational view of Oppenheim's? No writer on these topics has ever denied that coercion has something to do with 'power', though the relatedness is usually unspecified and merely assumed. Perhaps this is so because our intuition tells us that coercion, in all its forms, is an expression of some kind of power. And, since coercion is always successful (otherwise it is merely 'attempted' coercion), it signifies a successful exercise of power and domination. As such, coercion implies a form of social control. Given this association, we may now turn to a descriptive analysis of an 'operational' view of coercion.

In Oppenheim's work specific references to coercion, either in concept or application, are minimal. He cites instances of coercion to exemplify ways of 'exercising control' or to identify certain values ascribable to such ways (like whether coercion is 'good', 'bad', and so on).[18] It is also clear that all instances of coercion are conceived to be exercises of control, but not all exercises of control are necessarily coercive. Influencing behavior by incentives, inducements, rewards, or the promise of benefits, gifts, offers, and so on are implied as being noncoercive exercises of control.[19]

'Exercising control' is understood only in a social sense. Hence, Oppenheim's concept of social control (and thus, of coercion) is distinguishable from other forms of control because its meaning is restricted to power relations and observable interactions between two or more actors. It is meant to exclude other ways in which behavior is influenced not involving the actions of other people in any operational sense (e.g., phobias, mechanical disabilities, and 'moral sense'—all influencing and controlling various behaviors— but not in the social sense intended by Oppenheim). From our previous study of Oppenheim's idea of 'relations of control', we may elicit an operational notion of what the elements of a coercive relation might be.[20]

Coercion, as an instance of exercising control, is a relational term involving at least one participant whose (non)performance of some action successfully controls an (in)action of someone else, with the qualification that the (in)action of the first party is the sufficient condition or cause of the (in)action of the second party, in one of two ways: by compelling its performance or by preventing it. (To compel the nonperformance of an action means the same thing as to prevent it; to prevent the nonperformance of some action is to compel its occurrence.)

Strictly speaking, we are not entitled to say much more about Oppenheim's conception of coercion because, already, we have said a good deal more than his writings offer. In what follows I shall attempt to develop the concept of coercion somewhat beyond what Oppenheim has done, but I will utilize the parts of his conceptual scheme that are helpful in constructing our own view of coercion. I will continue to use, for the sake of brevity, the symbolic language as follows: P compels Q to do q or prevents Q from doing q, that is, the compelling or preventing action of P is a sufficient condition for Q's response. 'P' and 'Q' are participants; 'q' is an action of Q; and 'p' is an action of P.

COERCIVE CONTROL RELATIONS

Compelling someone to do something as coercion: Suppose P compels or makes it necessary or mandatory for Q to do q. Is this type of 'social control' relation invariably coercive?

Compelling someone may mean 'physically forcing'. In that case, Q's attempt not to do q (i.e., resisting) is unsuccessful owing to the sufficiently forceful physical action, p, of P. Q's unsuccessful resistance to P qualifies this relation as paradigmatically coercive because P, despite Q's resistance, manipulates Q's body and so causes Q to act in a specific manner. Of course, if Q attempted no resistance whatsoever against P's action, then, since no objective response action by Q to P's action was attempted, the relation is noncoercive because it lacks the objectively necessary 'action' elements. Only 'actions', and not mere movements, constitute coercion. Passive resistance like

Mahatma Gandhi's tactics in India against the British occupation forces is an action despite its passivity; however, a more subtle analysis than the present 'objectivist' one is needed to exhibit the nature of this type of 'action'. Physically forcing is, in this view, a way to coercively constrain someone's behavior by making it unavoidable or necessary to do something.

However, constraining or compelling Q to do q may also mean P's closing all preexisting alternatives open to Q except the one taken by Q. In all such cases, P manipulates Q's environment (and not Q's body) thereby making it necessary for Q to do q as a result of P's doing p. Constraining actions become coercive when: (1) they close all possible courses of action (q, non-q) otherwise open to Q, which Q has already chosen to pursue; and (2) the closure amounts to a sufficient condition of Q's doing q.[21]

We are to be reminded that, before we draw an equation between 'constraints' and 'coercive constraints' on the assumption that closure refers only to blocking or physical closure, there are any number of ways and means to close alternatives, ranging perhaps from threats of evil to blocking. However, only those 'coercive' constraints for which there is objectifiable evidence qualify for consideration.

The term 'coercion' may, in this view, be construed to mean not only compelling ('P physically forcing Q to do q' and 'P constraining Q to do q') but also preventing Q from doing q.

Preventing someone from doing something as coercion: 'P's restraining Q from doing q' is a form of preventing. A 'restraining relation' refers to the situation where Q tries to do q but fails as a consequence of P's intentional action, p. In order for 'P to restrain Q from doing q' in the stipulated sense, the pursuit of q must constitute a course of action objectively open to Q that becomes deliberately closed by the action, p, of P.

Of course, there are a multitude of ways for one participant to be restrained by another: P may physically frustrate or prevent Q's effort to do q, or else P may restrain Q's doing q by putting obstacles in Q's way or by making it disvaluable or unacceptably and deliberately risky for Q to do q so that, for practical purposes, Q is left with no choice except to stop trying to do, or pursue, q.

'Restraining' relations are a form of preventing, whereas 'preventing' may or may not indicate 'restraint' actions. The prime

difference is that Q tries unsuccessfully to do q when P restrains Q
from doing q. However, when P prevents Q from doing q, Q may
or may not try to do q. For instance, by placing barbed wire around
his or her property, the owner prevents the intrusion of the casual
trespasser, though no one may have yet tried to do so.

'Restraining actions' are coercive when Q's pursuing or
attempting to pursue q as a result of choice is made practically
impossible mainly as a consequence of P's doing p. Coercive
restraints are the most readily understood and practiced instances
of a participant's exercising control over the behavior of another,
besides 'compelling' relations.

In Oppenheim's objectivist view, restraining and constraining
interactive relations are, as a rule, coercive. But when P controls
Q's doing or not doing q, 'control' relations like these may be the
result chiefly of influence and not of restraint or constraint.
Sometimes it is difficult to decide whether, in specific situations,
P's action is an instance of influencing or of coercively restraining
because both types of control relations exist in degrees that blend
into one another. Oppenheim's concept of social control, as we
noted, includes only influence and coercive restraint as its
subclasses. In the negative sense, P controls Q's not doing q to the
degree that P influences Q not to do q or restrains Q from doing q.
In the positive sense, P controls Q's doing q to the extent that P
influences or constrains Q to do q.[22]

AUTONOMY, NOT FREEDOM

So far we have said nothing more about the abridgement of the
victim's (or coercee's) freedom, which many believe is the crux of
someone's being coerced. The question about whether the common
idea of coercion essentially concerns some serious loss of the
victim's preexisting freedom is answered in Oppenheim's analysis,
for it follows that it is the coercee's autonomy, and not freedom,
that suffers (or suffers most directly) in coercive relations.
Coercion can be posited as the most severe form of social control[23]
because it constitutes, in this view, a complete negation of social
autonomy. (For example, 'injuring', 'maiming,' 'threatening', are
all instruments of coercion.) Limitations on social freedom, on the
other hand, need not involve undercutting autonomy (as we have

shown in our discussion of 'unfreedom' relations) because Q can be both unfree (i.e., Q's freedom can be limited by P) and autonomous in his or her relationship with P.

On the conceptual level, when a relationship between two participants is characterized by either 'control' (influence, restraint, constraint) or 'autonomy' (the lack of control), we always know something about the actual behavior of the participants. With social freedom, this information is unavailable until after the action is performed. It is the crucial distinction between influence and restraint that manifests the connection between social freedom and control. By influencing Q not to do q (regardless of whether it is by means of dissuasion, deterrence, or conditioning), P controls Q's not doing q but does not limit his or her freedom to do it. Conversely, in P's restraining (in the sense of coercing) Q from doing q, P not only controls Q's not doing q but makes Q unfree (by prevention) to do q.

In general, coercive control (restraint/prevention, constraint/compulsion) limits the coercee's social freedom (and we would know this to be so, objectively) with respect to particular participants and their actions. Other forms of control do not necessarily do so (nor do we know beforehand which alternative Q will ultimately select). Therefore, freedom can coexist with control (influencing, but not coercive) relations, but autonomy (or lacking control) cannot. In this analytical scheme all autonomous actions are socially free actions, but not all free actions are autonomous. Neither is freedom the opposite of control, inasmuch as both relations can characterize a pair of participants simultaneously. Social autonomy and social freedom are not synonyms, for only freedom in the technical sense may be compatible with a control relation; autonomy never is.

In summary, coercive control (as well as all other types of 'control' relations) is absolutely incompatible with the autonomy of a participant in a power relationship. Coercive control also limits the social freedom of the coercee, but, obviously, not all restrictions are the result of coercion, or even of control, because it is conceivable that a participant is autonomous and yet unfree (where P makes it punishable for Q to do q) with respect to another in the relationship. And, finally, freedom does not always presuppose autonomy (though autonomy presupposes freedom) because, by implication, an overall gain in social freedom is not directly proportional in all cases to the maximization of social autonomy.

The objectivist framework for the concepts of autonomy, freedom, and coercion, which we have just presented, may be augmented in certain key respects with the intersubjective approach. In my view some of the important differences between these approaches will amplify the insights intersubjectivity brings to some unclear or incomplete conceptions and general problems arising in the 'objective' view and will add to our overall understanding of the complexities or subtleties of 'coercion' and its interconnections with the concept of autonomy.

First, with respect to the nonempirical meanings of 'freedom' and 'autonomy', we may claim that, of all possible senses in which these terms have been understood by us all, most are clearly unamenable to strict objectivist examination. Accordingly, it is a mistake to restrict usage only to those meanings that fit the objectivist approach or to fashion those meanings solely within the objectivist framework because, in the main, it ignores if not distorts our ordinary grasp of these nonobjective terms and imposes a too-arbitrary reductionistic limitation upon the meaning and scope of 'coercion'. But it also suggests, in contrast, that 'subjective' realities are both 'less real' (perhaps 'illusory', 'nonexistent', 'nothing but', and so on) and uninfluential in the determination of behavior and relations, which is not at all the case as we have been arguing in this volume. 'Freedom', in the ordinary sense, may mean 'being able to think certain thoughts or any thoughts of one's own at all when and as one wishes'; to act in given ways without external interference; or, perhaps, to *feel* free'; it may refer to an abstract moral ideal or reality (e.g., a condition or quality of personhood or certain conditions and relations between persons (and perhaps their God), states, corporate entities, and so on, as defined by law, politics, cultural tradition, or society in general. There are significant 'subjective' meanings and aspects of all ordinary senses adduced above. The need to define 'freedom' and 'autonomy' in objective terms does not necessarily include these senses. Indeed, they receive a nonstandard account, which, on its face, is not altogether objectionable, but rather incomplete (from the intersubjective viewpoint).

Intersubjectively understood, 'freedom' and 'autonomy' are defined as facets of a broader field of inquiry, including many subjective factors bearing on coercive relations and the conceptual meaning of coercion. For example, forming intentions, having and expressing beliefs, acting with motives, making choices, exercising 'will', 'inner meaning' constitution, all become living and lived realities of experience instead of merely being supposed by logical inference, external 'evidence', and operational criteria, as the objectivist viewpoint propounds. Therefore, when we assert that 'with respect to P, Q is socially free', we may mean at least two different things: the opposite of 'not being free' and feeling free—both being equally 'factual', 'rational', 'causal', and important. The first meaning may be specified in objective terms, while the second meaning is obviously subjective. The key difference in approach here between the objectivist and the inter-subjectivist is that for the latter, the factuality, rationality, and causal significance of 'feeling free', particularly in the context of social relations and interactions, can become a serious factor in the overall understanding of a set of events in question and would only be swept aside by any exclusive consideration of the objective side. Again, this is not an argument against scientific 'objectivity' in the study of the social world but for the rejection of the strict 'objectivist' theory of social science.

Second, the putative value-neutrality claimed by the objectivist for his or her concepts of freedom, autonomy, and coercion is *not* an unreasonable ideal incompatible with the intersubjective view being advanced here. Indeed, intersubjectivity can, where a question of values is concerned (either with respect to the subject or object of inquiry), acknowledge and describe the relevant values in terms of their nature and influence on the process and 'findings' of inquiry; it does not merely proceed to rule them out of any integral consideration. A simple objective definition of 'autonomy' or 'freedom' has been the 'absence of coercion'. The presence of coercion, on the other hand, has meant the 'absence of freedom and/or autonomy'. Further inquiry shows the inadequacy of this definition, owing not to its value-freedom but to its highly abstract formulation. Oppenheim's theory at least offers us a set of 'operational' definitions with a supposedly greater power of dis-crimination and application, since we know beforehand the different ways some actor's freedom or autonomy can be abridged or enlarged in the relevant sense.

But both 'objective' definitions fail to deal with values in an important sense. Take the coercion and suicide example cited in note 21 in this chapter. In symbolic language, it is a case where P coercively constrains Q to do q because P diminishes Q's freedom and autonomy in a certain determinate manner (i.e., in operational terms, by closing the other alternatives, in this case making it more disvaluable to pursue them than the one—q—desired by P and also by making the closure sufficient for Q's doing q), even in the extreme instance where Q chooses suicide, q, over P's threat to torture Q to death.

Now, Q may have decided that, under these circumstances, q was the prudential thing to do. Even if this act of prudence was dictated by subjective preference (taste or value), the objectivist would nevertheless regard P's coercive relation to Q as determinable in objective terms alone, not because the distinction between prudence and preference can be objectively shown[24] but mainly due to P's action being a sufficient cause of Q's doing q. Both are 'observables' even though strictly speaking (following the classic theory of David Hume), the causal nexus is not. Hence, in this view, any role 'value' that may have contributed to the relation between P and Q is eliminated. Also, freedom and autonomy are held to be abridged, not because the abridgment is 'observable', but because Q's doing q is not truly Q's own action as it would *presumably* have been without P's threatening action making it necessary for Q to do q.

But Q's prudential action may indeed reduce to value-preference, and so, in any final tally on coercion, the subjective factor of Q's inner life (namely, his taste, hierarchy of values, and so on) may figure prominently. For instance, neither death nor torture may be the most serious evils many perceive them to be, for yielding to the torturer's demand to reveal one's secrets may be of less value to some (admittedly many fewer) people than enduring intense pain and suffering in silence. Furthermore, although the notion of the actions of rational agency depends upon the distinction between prudence and personal desire or taste, the objectivist's effort to cite some universal evils (like torture, intense pain, death, loss of property, and so on) is not always likely to yield the same clearly 'objective' outcome hoped for, insofar as not nearly everyone (dis)values these things equally under all possible circumstances. Thus, these subjective 'value' differences (even at different times in a single person's life) may contribute as importantly to 'Q's doing q' as P's action does.

The intersubjectivist, on the other hand, does have a rational understanding of 'the subjective' because his or her perspective is one that understands in the most basic way the distinction between subjectivity and objectivity in the first place. In short, he recognizes the limitations inherent in the objective point of view as seen from the broader context of society and social experience (including 'values', 'meanings', and other subjective phenomena of participants as well as 'observers').

The third difference between the objectivist and intersubjectivist is an extension of the second. It is drawn with respect to *what* the objectivist cannot give an adequate accounting where the intersubjectivist can.

In general, we observe that every subjectively determined phenomenon does not necessarily have an objective-behavioral counterpart, for example, many of our feelings and thoughts remain forever a part of our inner life. It is also true that, without an accompanying subjective state, no behavior is understandable; in fact, no 'behavior' as such is possible, only physical movement is possible in response to physical stimuli. From the standpoint of the objectivist, except by inference, no objectifiable knowledge of effective choice supposedly prior to an action taken on its behalf is available. The intersubjectivist understands subjectivity, in his or her own case, immediately; but he or she can also comprehend 'from the inside', so to speak, the meaning of effective choice as a subjective reality in the lives of others, while he or she can simultaneously interpret objective 'evidence'. I will return to this point shortly.

There is a perspective that is *internal* to a given social situation, that is, from the point of view of the participants. I refer to the type of relationship involving the participants, their definition of the relation or situation, and the subjective meaning the relation has for them in terms of the roles assumed by the parties of the relation that ultimately and mainly prompt and explain consequent behavior. The objectivist does not regard this perspective as significant because it is nonobjectifiable. The intersubjectivist does regard this perspective as significant because he recognizes that, in the context of role-structured social relations (either predetermined for, or constituted by, the actor), there are relative and shifting spheres of autonomy relations the objectivist cannot understand. But it is the presence or absence of such spheres of autonomy that is the single most significant variable in determining the fact and degree of coerciveness of a given social relation.

Now, we can resume the discussion that we left dangling above. Certain role-relationships and role-perceptions may definitively influence the orientation and courses of action of participants with respect to each other in a social situation. The 'objective behavior' can be fully grasped, in addition to the objectivity of events, only if we know the personal and/or group meanings bestowed on the events in question by the participants as well as observers and the interpretations they give to their involvements. For example, if 'freedom' is defined as the availability and capacity to exercise effective choice,[25] the mere fact that P compels Q to act against his or her will does not by this alone make Q a victim of a coercive denial of freedom (i.e., by rendering choice-making ineffective). In competitive sports relationships between players (which are nonetheless power relationships despite the fact they are played in accord with rules for fun or business), knowledge of context, tactics, and goals, and knowledge of the players' intentions, and not only their actions, will contribute to our overall understanding of the events taking place before our eyes and to the definition of the situation. Without full knowledge of the 'internal' perspective I spoke of earlier, very little sense can be made of the 'observables' alone. The football player, in the case of a competitive sport, may resist the exercise of choice to score a touchdown or be tackled by the opposition. Unless we understand that what we observe is a sport and possess knowledge of its rules and some insight as to the player's intentions, choices, and so on, this relation (between the player and the opposition) would be described by the objectivist—who relies solely on 'observables'—as a coercive one.[26] The intersubjectivist would describe it differently, or, if not altogether differently, the subjective dimension would, when suitable, acquire a significance foreclosed upon by the objectivist (suitability would be determined *after* the event and upon examination). Indeed, the intersubjective perspective is so basic and pervasive that its existence and impact upon our process of experience is too easily overlooked.

To review, the intersubjectivist accepts the view that the autonomy of participants (and of their social freedom) may also be defined in terms of the social relations in which each stands to, and interacts with, the other. In this sense, 'intersubjective' autonomy (and freedom) is not only relative to a particular social situation but to a perspective internal to the situation as well, namely, the relevant view and perceptions that the participants have of themselves and of others involved. The intersubjectivist rejects the extreme notion that both human autonomy and social freedom are universal abstractions referring to the relationless condition or property of individual human beings. Therefore, coercion cannot be construed, in my view, simply as an encroachment upon social autonomy—in the *abstract* sense. It also rejects, as I have been suggesting, the objectivist concepts of autonomy and freedom owing to the objectivist's principled and methodological exclusion of subjective factors.

The logic of the view I defend permits us to accept that, although a participant's autonomy (in either the abstract or the objectivist sense) is infringed by another party to the relation, the type of social role that may engage the participants compels us to deny any putative coerciveness of the existing social relation because their spheres of autonomy *relative to each other* (or should we say the victim's autonomy understood intersubjectively) remain uninfluenced or at least not diminished by the one's interactive relation with respect to the other. Coercion means a forfeiture or diminution of autonomy, as understood in the broader context of social relations of exercising power and control, including 'the subjective' and 'internal meanings' related to the context.

How do we frame the concept of autonomy in the terms of intersubjectivity? It is hoped that the outcome will provide a new, nonempirical definition of these terms, one that denies any final radical dichotomy between the objective and subjective realms of reality while at the same time broadening the scope of scientific inquiry beyond what the objectivist's perspective allows. In this sense, then, I intend that my definition of coercion does not reject but builds upon Oppenheim's philosophy in order to complete it.

To this we add the general observation that the intersubjective perspective should not be expected usually to yield claims about specific instances of coercion always at variance with the objectivist's. In fact, they will typically agree provided that all relevant determinants of a (social) control relationship are specified. The same reasoning holds for 'autonomy' and 'social freedom' in the limited sense that coercion receives its concept from them in terms of the sorts of social relations that define them. These relations, as we have said, are not always specifiable on 'objective' grounds alone.

The intersubjective approach to social autonomy helps us to define both the nature of autonomy and the coercive infringements on autonomy, though I believe the most abstract definition of autonomy is fundamentally the same whether we approach it operationally or intersubjectively, namely, the denial of a social control relationship between two or more participants in the context of a power relation. However, if actions speak for themselves, then, mere observation could decide the presence or absence of a control relation in the requisite sense; the introduction of intersubjectivity would, insofar as the scientific endeavor is concerned, be pointless. But since an interpretation of actions raises the question of context of both 'interpretation' and occurrence of actions, it is realistic to consider the relevant 'observables' in conjunction with the nonempirical phenomena.

Take the case of 'the outstretched hand,' perhaps seen by the two participants as a (gesture of) salutation. It is not perceived and interpreted by them as simply a physical or anatomical event, but it has a 'meaning' one participant conveys to another. The other, of course, understands the meaning of the gesture, i.e., it is an expression of the one's intention and expectation with respect to the other. The mere concurrence of viewpoints between participants is also not sufficient to render the event ('the outstretched hand') as being 'objective' without also giving due consideration to its subjective meaning. Again, the subtlety of intersubjective meaning in the definition of a situation or an event must not remain unaccounted for.

But since an interpretation of actions, events, and participants is made by the external observer—from the standpoint of observation—it must include in its final formation full consideration of all relevant factors internal to the social relation, namely, the motives, intentions, and roles of the participants, or the subjective meaning each's involvement has with and for the others. These must be disclosed in order to establish the absence of a control relation and posit the existence of an 'autonomy' relation between participants (i.e., in which each is socially autonomous with regards to the other).

In an informal social setting, role relationships are usually less structured and thus more spontaneity of interaction occurs. Often it is the *interpreted* intention of a participant in a social scene that prompts another's behavior towards that participant. For instance, your date holds open a door and in so doing signals for you to pass through first. This event is interpretatively inseparable from the door-holder's intention to be polite. Divested of the door-holder's intention, the act is merely an objective, physical series of events. Suppose now that the door-holder is a known gangster to whom Q owes money long past due, Q's interpretation of the gangster's act may prompt Q to enter only *after* the door-holder does. In this situation it matters if participant Q's walking through the door as a result of P's holding it open is done by Q because of an 'implied threat' (perhaps an instrument of coercion); or if Q refuses to enter until P does; or if Q's entering is due to no control exercised at all, i.e., because the door was opened from a motive of politeness and Q would have done as he or she did anyway in 'polite' response. In the first two instances, the order of entry is a result of influence and control (though our description of the second requires qualification); in the last instance the order of entry is not a result of influence and control, and so the autonomy of Q with respect to P is, at least in this instance, preserved. These are not, of course, necessarily coercive events. Calling them such would depend in the second instance on whether Q's refusal to enter before P is a (refusal to comply) response to P's 'implied threat' (for if so, and this is the qualification, it is P's 'failure to control' Q); and in the first instance, the coerciveness of the relation hinges on the degree to which P's action constrains Q to do as he or she does.[27]

It is from the intersubjective viewpoint, and not from the objectivist's, that we are *theoretically* enabled to understand the nature of social autonomy, particularly in some cases where, as we have noted before, the social relation is defined by 'relative and shifting spheres of autonomy' (sometimes conditioned by 'sub-

jective' causes but chiefly conditioned by the role relations
between participants). Obviously, the implication is that if no
autonomy relationship exists prior to the interaction between two
participants, we cannot impute 'coercion' to the resulting social
relation once we define coercion as an infringement on a
participant's social autonomy.[28]

'Objective' accounts of spheres of social autonomy are only one
aspect of the whole story because they cannot comprehend, in the
light of the concept of 'spheres of autonomy', the nonobjectifiable
dimension that may, as I indicate in my examples above, make the
difference in classifying or assessing a relationship rightly as to its
coerciveness.

DEFINITION OF SOCIAL AUTONOMY

In the context of social power, social autonomy may be defined
intersubjectively as relative and shifting spheres of autonomy in
terms of which there are no control relations between the
participants, who remain socially free with respect to one another
as they exercise their own self-chosen pursuits in accord with their
life-plans. These spheres or dynamic boundaries are determined in
both their subjective and objective aspects by social roles and
structures, institutions of law, economics, politics, and culture, by
history, ideology, consensus, and/or by purely personal definition.
In my view there is no non-social meaning of autonomy as I intend
it in an analysis of coercion. All coercion situations occur in a
relational context.

Moreover, only in the most abstract formulation are we able to
consider 'social autonomy' as a distinctly nonnormative concept.
Its 'nonnormativeness' we predicate simply on the ground that on
this level no inherent 'value' accrues to the fact of whether or not
'social control' is absent in a particular social relationship. But
once we consider autonomy and control relations in terms of
practical social and personal realities (like age, customs,
competence, role-relations of participants), 'value' is too closely
interwoven on this level to regard social autonomy and its coercive
diminishment as value-neutral or nonnormative.

I shall not further encumber the discussion with specific references to the intersubjective dimension of social freedom for the reason that social autonomy has been shown to be the more central concept in our understanding of coercion.

Before we explain how, in contrast to Oppenheim's philosophy, the nonempirical or intersubjective definitions of autonomy and coercion plug into our format, I must comment on a noticeable exclusion from the list of social institutions above, namely, the institutions of religion and morality. I do not intend to deny their enormous influence and importance on the ways in which we conceive and decide matters of human autonomy, freedom, and coercion. My concern is restricted to an analysis of the elements, features, and conditions relative to a social concept of coercion. Insofar as religion and morality introduce 'revelations' and 'truths' that are not of genuine social origin and explication, then, no matter how enlightened their claims may prove to be, a consideration of them lies beyond the scope of the present task. To be sure, participants in social relations (individuals, groups, corporations, and so on) may perform actions and relate to others on the basis of, for example, religious and moral motives and roles, and so to the degree these constitute a social causal-explanation, they become relevant in our analysis. I had merely hoped to avoid the connotations of 'otherworldliness' in dissociating my analysis from these institutions as they are commonly understood.

THE NEW DEFINITION OF COERCION

My definition of coercion builds upon Oppenheim's. For him, the term 'coercion' may be defined as a control relation between P and Q where P's doing p (or even P him or herself) is the primary cause of Q's (not) doing q.

We may plug his definition into our format as follows:

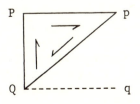

Before P can coerce Q, however, an autonomy relationship must preexist P's attempt to control Q or Q's behavior, that is, Q's autonomy consists in Q's being able to control his or her own behavior with respect to P; and P's autonomy refers to controlling his or her own affairs in relation to q. Social autonomy is a necessary condition for coercion. In brief, Oppenheim's definition corresponds to the main 'objective' ECs in my format: two participants together with their interrelated behaviors, where p is the coercing instrument of P, and q is the coerced behavior of Q.

Although the definition of coercion we have supposed for Oppenheim constitutes the 'operationalized' elements of coercion, in the last analysis it is a static and segmented view of what actually takes place. To improve upon his definition, our own must comprehend the dynamic nature of social [role] relations and with it the participant's relative and shifting spheres of autonomy that, after all, are determining factors for coercion. By including the ECs of Oppenheim's philosophy, his becomes a springboard to our own intersubjective approach.

In my own view, the constellation of Oppenheim's ECs occurs in a *role context*, which in turn explains how social power relations come into play between participants, and thence, how coercion evolves as a dynamic interactive relation. Clearly, the static approach of the operational view does not disclose how a social role may structure and modify the participants' interrelations and so account for changing degrees of coercion ranging from Q's diminishing control over q because of P or something P does or does not do, to Q's becoming an instrument of P's control as P increases his or her autonomy over Q's (not) doing q.

The notion of power here is very important because the growing and diminishing spheres of autonomy of the participants, P and Q, discussed earlier, are crucial in establishing what 'power' means. And, reciprocal and respective ranges of autonomy set the tone for whether any particular control relation is coercive.

In the preceding chapter I examined such key nonobjective terms as 'will', 'choice', 'consent', 'intention', and so on, intersubjectively. By 'choice' we mean that Q's freedom to (not) do q is always established in Q's relationship to P and the range of autonomy it allows for Q to (not) do q, q^1, q^2, and so on. Hence the relationship between P and Q is very significant, especially if it involves a situation of P's building up power over Q's range of autonomy. The concept of will means that P has autonomy over doing p and Q over doing q. In P's coercion of Q, Q does or does not do q against Q's will as P imposes his or her own will over Q's autonomy in doing what he or she does under coercion, and so on. Each of these terms has some significant bearing on the social autonomy of the participants.

My definition of coercion includes not only the ECs in Oppenheim's definition (the participants and their respective behaviors), but it also recognizes the 'p' of P as an instrument of coercion, as it recognizes the crucial role aspects of the participant's relationship together with the relative and shifting spheres of autonomy that condition the possibility of coercion in the first place.

The language of our symbolic format now may be used to express how the two correlative units of social analysis that we have introduced, social role ('R') and social autonomy, may be classified in our scheme. R belongs not to any particular EC in itself (i.e., $EC^{x \cdots n}$) because it is neither a constant nor variable feature of P, Q, p, or q taken separately. Instead, R, along with *its* essential but variable feature, autonomy, forms the contextual structure of the definition of the conceptual relationship between the ECs; in addition, the development of a coercive e/r ('event/relationship') can occur only as R sets the terms for interaction between the participants.

I propose the following definition of coercion, using the Ps and Qs of my format: Q is coerced by P when P causes Q to relinquish his or her known and valued autonomy over him or herself in some limited respect, for example, over Q's (not) doing q by controlling Q's (not) doing q. This definition covers both physical and nonphysical types of coercion.

In this definition social autonomy is both an essential feature and a necessary condition of coercion. At the outset of coercion, P must have autonomy over p, and Q over q. As P's instrument of coercion, p must be fully under P's control; and q must be under Q's control. q must actually occur. Thus, for the occurrence of each act of coercion, the following must happen. p is an instrument of coercion, the means by which P seeks to extend his or her power and autonomy over Q in some respect. The concept of force is not the instrument itself but rather the *measure* of the instrument of coercion. p must be sufficiently known to Q to represent a sign to Q to permit Q to relinquish his or her autonomy over q at the time. Q knows that p is an instrument of coercion and so understands the changes his or her relationship with P is undergoing. P and Q do not have overlapping spheres of autonomy with regard to q. Q objects both to what he or she is (not) made to do under coercion and also to being made an instrument of P.

To the extent that Q or Q's (not) doing q continues to be an instrument of P, P no longer really coerces Q in this respect but simply comes to dominate Q in a total power relationship. In effect, by losing a sufficient range of his or her autonomy to P, q or Q becomes an extension of P or of P's autonomy.

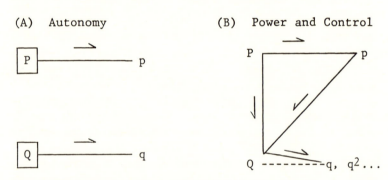

(A)   Autonomy   (B)   Power and Control

Each participant in A has autonomy over his or her own affairs with respect to the other. In B, P assumes power over Q's doing q.

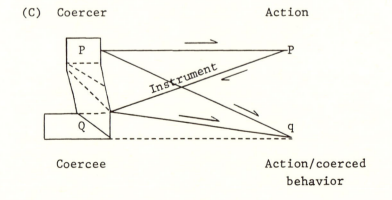

(C)   Coercer   Action

Coercee   Action/coerced
                                      behavior

In the next chapter I will illustrate the power of my definition by applying it to two examples of the dynamic and relational view of coercion.

NOTES

1. See Harry Frankfurt, "Coercion and Moral Responsibility," in *Essays on Freedom of Action*, Ted Honderich, ed. (London: Routledge and Kegan Paul, 1973), p. 83. See also Felix Oppenheim in his *The Dimensions of Freedom* (New York: St. Martin's Press, 1970), passim.

2. For example, see Robert Paul Wolff, *In Defense of Anarchism* (New York: Harper and Row, 1970), pp. 12-13. Also see Isaiah Berlin, *Four Essays on Liberty* (New York: Oxford University Press, 1970), p. 137; and John Churchill, "Coercion and the Authority of Reason." *Metaphilosophy* 15 (July/October 1984), p. 181.

3. Gerald Dworkin, "Autonomy and Behavior Control," in *Interpretation and Reflection: Basic Issues in Medical Ethics,* 2d edition, Ronald Munson, ed. (Belmont, Calif.: Wadsworth, 1983), p. 332.

4. For example, see Mortimer Adler's *The Idea of Freedom,* vols. 1 and 2 (Westport, Conn.: Greenwood Press, 1976).

5. Oppenheim describes his task as a value-free nonnormative approach to social freedom; he implies the same about autonomy. However, he rejects the view that social freedom (and likewise, autonomy) has no meaningful and important normative implications. Autonomy and freedom are unlike the concepts in Chapter 3 because of the primary social values they commonly convey. Coercion and freedom are often tied in in the following way by a majority of philosophers: freedom is at least the absence of coercion (e.g., Cheney Ryan, "The Normative Concept of Coercion," *Mind* 89 [October 1980], p. 482; and Berlin, *Four Essays on Liberty*, p. 122; H.L.A. Hart, "Are There Any Natural Rights?", in *Human Rights,* A. I. Melden, ed. [Belmont, Calif.: Wadsworth, 1970], p. 61), and *unfreedom* is crucial to a full understanding of coercion as a social phenomenon. For instance, as another contemporary philosopher Robert Nozick has observed, a full study of freedom will involve "reasons which justify making someone unfree to perform an action" as well as "the reason why making someone unfree to perform an action needs justifying." Nozick further states that although coercion does not exhaust the notion of unfreedom, there is a definite relationship between coercion and unfreedom. (Robert Nozick, "Coercion," in Sidney Morgenbesser, Patrick Suppes, and Morton White, eds., *Philosophy, Science and Method* [New York: St. Martin's Press, 1969], p. 440; also Bernard Gert, "Coercion and Freedom," in *Coercion: NOMOS XIV,* J. R. Pennock and

J. W. Chapman, eds. [Chicago: Aldine-Atherton Press, 1972] pp. 30-48.)
Oppenheim simply wishes to distinguish between its value-free and value-
laden senses because value-influence is unscientific.

6. For instance, a dependent power and unfreedom relationship can
exist between a pair of agents, and still one may be both free (i.e., can
choose to do or not do something the other makes punishable) and
autonomous (i.e., Y has power over X's doing x but refuses to exercise it by
influencing or restraining/constraining X's behavior).

7. Oppenheim, *Dimensions of Freedom*, pp. 7, 14, 110.

8. Oppenheim calls this "exercising control," ibid., p. 28.

9. Ibid., pp. 43, 100.

10. That is, to influence or restrain someone's action but not necessarily
to limit freedom of action in some way—to make it unfree or punishable.

11. Oppenheim, *Dimensions of Freedom*, pp. 64, n.6, 100. But the status
of a 'disposition', like a 'tendency', is not at all objectifiable, apart from
the behaviors they supposedly manifest.

12. All alternatives are intentionally closed to the controllee except one
(constraining): the closing of a previously open alternative course of action
to the controllee (restraining); also see, Oppenheim, *Dimensions of
Freedom,* pp. 25, 26.

13. 'Failure to control' is different from 'no control', for example,
where a response action is absent. If a police officer drags a striking worker
to jail, the officer 'acts', whereas the worker moves or is being moved. The
officer does not control the striker's behavior, in Oppenheim's view,
because the response action, i.e., the element of choice on the part of the
striker, is lacking. The striker chose neither to comply with nor to resist the
officer's action.

14. Oppenheim, *Dimensions of Freedom,* pp. 111, 117; in Oppenheim's
view, a distinction exists between 'freedom' and 'enabling' (or 'giving
opportunity to'): the failure to make it possible or to enable someone to do
something is not necessarily an instance of preventing or making it
impossible for him or her to do it; there is no unfreedom relation here (p.
120). If X's doing x is unavoidable for reasons not linked with actions of
any agent in particular, X is (by definition) free (or not) to do x. For
example, poor people are free to become rich; they lack only the
opportunity.

15. For example, *John Locke: Two Treatises of Government,* P. Laslett,
ed. (Cambridge: Cambridge University Press, 1963), pp. 311, 328, 352;
Chapter 4, sec. 22; Chapter 6, sec. 57. Also, for a discussion of Kant in this
regard, see David Gauthier, *Practical Reasoning* (Oxford: Oxford at the
Clarendon Press, 1963), pp. 111-13, 191. And, for Mill, see Berlin, *Four
Essays on Liberty,* pp. 124-27; also see Hay's discussion of Rawls: Joyce B.

Hay, "Three Conceptions of Autonomy in Rawls' Theory of Justice," *Midwest Studies in Philosophy* 2 (1977), pp. 62, 65-67, 75; Thomas Scanlon, "A Theory of Expression," in *The Philosophy of Law,* Ronald M. Dworkin, ed. (New York: Oxford University Press, 1977), pp. 153-71; Sharon Hill Bishop, "Self-Determination and Autonomy" in *Today's Moral Problems,* R. Wasserstrom, ed. (New York: Macmillan, 1979), pp. 118-33; and S. I. Benn, "Freedom, Autonomy, and the Concept of a Person," *Proceedings of the Aristotelian Society* 76 (1975-76), pp. 109-30.

16. For examples, see Richard Flathman, *The Practice of Rights* (Cambridge: Cambridge University Press, 1976), pp. 157, 165, 186, 188; and Jeffrie Murphy, "Rights and Borderline Cases," *Arizona Law Review* 19, 228 (1978), pp. 231, 235-36.

17. See Ronald M. Dworkin, "Liberalism," in *Public and Private Morality,* Stuart Hampshire, ed. (Cambridge: Cambridge University Press, 1979), p. 143; also see R. M. Dworkin's *Taking Rights Seriously* (Cambridge, Mass.: Harvard University Press, 1977), pp. 169, 172, 176, 182, 239, 269, 272-74, 277.

18. Oppenheim, *Dimensions of Freedom,* pp. 55, 224-26.

19. The noncoerciveness of any and all of these is not at all obvious, as the debate on 'coercive offers' shows: see David Zimmerman "Coercive Wage Offers," *Philosophy and Public Affairs* 10 (Spring 1981), pp. 121-45; Lawrence Alexander, "Zimmerman on Coercive Wage Offers," *Philosophy and Public Affairs* (April 1983), pp. 160-71; and Virginia Held, "Coercion and Coercive Affairs," in *Coercion*, Pennock and Chapman, eds., p. 57.

20. The operational approach has been seriously criticized by some others, most notably Cheyney Ryan in "The Normative Concept of Coercion," *Mind* 89 (October 1980). In response to Ryan's critique, Patrick Wilson seeks to reclaim the nonnormative view of coercion by maintaining that it has to do solely with overcoming resistance by force, in "Ryan on Coercion," *Mind* 91 (April 1982), p. 263, and *passim.*

21. A case where even suicide is compatible with coercion, which shows this clear causal relation between P and Q, is as follows: P is a known tyrant; Q is his or her prisoner and is told by P to kill him or herself and that unless Q does, P will torture Q to death. Q kills him or herself to avoid a painful and slow death. This example is also cited by William Tolhurst, in "Suicide, Self-sacrifice and Coercion," *The Southern Journal of Philosophy* 21, 1 (Spring 1983), pp. 114-15.

22. Oppenheim, *Dimensions of Freedom,* pp. 37, 46.

23. Punishment is sometimes confused with coercive control. The need for punishment signifies a failure to control someone's action and so is not an instrument of control.

24. For an elaboration of this distinction on ostensibly 'objective' grounds, see Mark Fowler, "Coercion and Practical Reason," *Social Theory and Practice* 8, 3 (Fall 1982), p. 332.

25. See Richard Norman, "Does Equality Destroy Liberty?" in *Contemporary Political Philosophy,* K. Graham, ed. (New York: Cambridge University Press, 1982), p. 90.

26. See Robert L. Simon, *Sports and Values* (Englewood Cliffs, N.J.: Prentice-Hall, 1985), pp. 53-57; Simon discusses where a line is to be drawn between violence and the use of force as well the ethics of violence in contact sports in general.

27. In theory, at least, the objectivist stance here seems unimpeachable because the objective causal link seems clear enough. However, Q's apparent capitulation may be due, not to P's action alone, but to Q's paranoidal tendency to avoid even the remotest possible disagreement. This, I suggest, unsettles the objectivist's basis because the causal nexus is predetermined only on the grounds of observable events. Psychological states as causes are unobjectifiable.

28. As individual human beings, the 'abstract autonomy' theorist might argue, their 'autonomy' preexists all social situations, and this factor overrides *prima facie* the particulars of any specific situation. The inter-subjectivist rebuttal denies any pre-social, pre-situational existence for persons, and any autonomy achieved is a result of a combination of individual and social factors.

CHAPTER 5

Coercion as a Dynamic Concept

If we were to regard coercion solely in terms of the elements of actions, participants, instruments, and the subjective features of will, choice, intention, and so on, we would commit a fallacy of mistaking the 'part' for the 'whole'. From these we cannot establish the existence of a coercive *relationship*, but merely coercive actions or instruments or coerced participants. In the presence of these one may infer the existence of a coercive relationship. And yet, some account must be offered of a type of relationship in which no specific actions or instruments are distinctly coercive and where the participants do not seem to be coerced but which is nevertheless coercive. The relative and shifting spheres of autonomy defining social relations will also help to define an important type of relationship, namely, role relations.

Accordingly, to describe dynamic social relationships that are or become coercive, the category of social role must be included now in our analysis.

In this section two different and highly publicized events will be used to exemplify the indispensable place of social role in an analysis of a coercive *relationship*. The first will be a largely fictionalized composite of events that occurred in the mid-1970s. It involved the abduction of a daughter of a wealthy and influential news mogul by a self-styled band of terrorists who sought to pressure authorities to release from prison two members of their band incarcerated for a 'political' murder. Though some parts of the following descriptive interpretations will ring true, I will purposely exaggerate certain occurrences and creatively construct others in order to amplify the points I wish to elucidate. The second example to be analyzed is the Cuban Missile Crisis. In this case I will stay as close to accurate portrayal as I can, since the relevant facts and events are sufficient for us to establish what we intend.

The analysis will be carried through from the perspective of the various roles of the chief players or participants involved. As each of these situations evolves, a diagram will be presented corresponding to the description of a given phase in the unfolding of events. The purpose behind the diagrams is to reveal the dynamic and relational nature of coercion by showing how changes in roles can affect the coerciveness of the respective relationships.

Relationships that are not role-based are excluded from consideration because these are better analyzed in terms of the elements and features cited above, since the type of relationship is inconsequential to the coercive interplay between participants.

EXAMPLE I: ABDUCTION

PHASE 1

Prior to the abduction, the victim neither knew or was in any way linked to her abductors. Nor was she sympathetic to the political views and aims of the band of terrorists. Thus, her initial response to her violent abduction was from fear for her own safety. In terms of our analysis no specific interconnected active role relationships are said to exist between the victim and her abductors. Both she and they were entirely free to act with regards to each other. At the precise moment she responds to the abduction attempt and either reluctantly submits or unsuccessfully resists the terrorists' actions, she enters a control relationship with them; she, of course, is the controllee, and they, the controllers.

In abducting their victim the terrorist band is fulfilling a self-appointed social role. They have perceptually constructed their own 'revolutionary' program, one phase of which calls for the dramatic abduction of this particular person. She, of course, has been coerced into becoming part of the *soi-disant* role her abductors have cast for themselves. Her behavior, in relation to them, is not at this point determinately role-based; theirs is. She neither accepts her role as victim nor, we can surmise, is she inspired by any particular role with attendant rights or responsibilities in response to the actions of her abductors. Presumably she was scared and helpless. The terrorists were intent on imposing upon their victim a prisoner-of-war status, which is a social role that its originators have invested with certain determinate expectations.

SUMMARY OF PHASE 1

In the earliest phase of this abduction, that is, when the victim is confronted by her kidnappers and their intentions are made manifest, a definite control relationship is established between them and her.

The Control Relationship

The success of the controller's exercise of power would be evidenced in the victim's leaving with them against her will. Suppose she resisted unsuccessfully. In this case her behavior was noncontributory to the outcome. If she simply submitted to the threats of her abductors or to their obvious physical and material (i.e., guns) superiority without resistance, then to some extent she contributed to the success of the effort of the abductors. Since the victim presumably would never have chosen to leave with her abductors independently, the terrorist band was, in the main, the foremost cause of her doing so. Hence, she becomes a party (as controllee) to the control relationship now established.

So far the participants have moved from action and interaction to a control and then coercive control relationship almost simultaneously.

A Coercive Control Relationship

By doing x (e.g., making threats, using physical violence, and so on), X forcibly compels Y to leave (y^2) her home without or against her consent; the victim's resistance (y^1) is short-lived and nugatory. Therefore, Y has minimal or no control over her doing y^2: X causes Y to do y^2 (but provokes y^1).

But this is not merely a control relationship (which it would be if X simply influenced Y to pursue the actions she took): it is a coercive one. Y has become a victim of coercion. The 'role' connection is as follows: X is a political terrorist group which uses

Y, a wholly innocent and unwilling party, to advance their own political program. To X, Y is a means by which they seek to achieve certain goals (though these may be revised in the course of acting out the group's destiny).

Coercion and the Deprivation of Social Autonomy

It may be supposed that the victim would escape or attempt to escape from her abductors if she believed her chance for success placed her at less risk than remaining in the role of prisoner of war as defined by her kidnappers. But she does not attempt escape and remains coercively controlled, and so without *social* autonomy with respect to the terrorists as well as to her everyday relationships. But we presume she retains, in a sense, a 'will of her own' as well as an intention to escape from those who have imprisoned her involuntarily.

In her coercive relationship with X, at least in its earliest phases, Y does what she does ostensibly to minimize possible harm. Though to the degree she, Y, can succeed in escaping from her status as prisoner of war, she reestablishes her social autonomy with regards to X.

PHASE 2

In this the second phase of the abduction, the victim, Y, is held in closely guarded quarters, unfree to remove herself from captivity. In the course of everyday necessities, she manages to develop a one-to-one or sub relationship with one of her captors, X^1. His view of Y simultaneously as victim, a 'means', and person in need of sympathy (perhaps X^1 also senses the possibility of 'reeducating' Y along programmatic lines) begins to transform certain aspects of their coercive social relationship. Sympathetic gestures gain increasing frequency as he does some decent things for his (group's) victim within the context of the overall 'coercion' relationship, for example, he allows her to express some of her feelings without excessive recrimination, gets her little things she needs to keep herself going, and even nurtures a personal liking for Y, but X^1 starts to use his position of power and control to persuade her of his 'good' intentions, despite his obvious role as abductor, captor, and political agent of his group's ideology.

X represents the terrorist group, and X^1 is one of its members. The diagram conveys that X^1 is largely but not entirely controlled in his actions by his group with respect to his relations with Y. In this diagram, Y begins to exert some control over her own actions, y (with respect to X^1 or X), though Y becomes in her actions increasingly an instrument of X^1 to the extent she adopts (*because* of her captivity, or because she is brainwashed and internalizes) X^1's ideology. As a consequence, the overt influence of X^1 (and gradually perhaps of X also) over Y and Y's doing y diminishes as Y assumes in part a new role with regards to her captors.

Y begins to see X^1 more as a person like herself, and not merely as her captor. In short, Y views X^1 on several different levels simultaneously, namely, as a 'means' of personal survival within the generally coercive control relationship; and, because we suppose that she has had aroused in her certain nascent feelings of sympathy and perhaps some personal affection for this specific member of the terrorist band, Y may also find herself drawn to the ideology that primarily motivates X^1. Consequently, not everything Y does that her captors demand or expect of her, in addition to her remaining generally docile and compliant, is of a forcibly coerced nature. Indeed, she may gradually curry favor with her "friendly" captor to convince him of her change in attitude and thus to catch the band off guard and escape with the help of X^1 or at least neutralize his response in the event of an escape attempt. However, not everything Y does now is performed with an eye towards escape.

PHASE 3

In this newest phase, the coercive relationship between the participants is transformed. It gives way to another sort of relationship owing to the alterations of role undergone by the victim. She assumes a new and different role redefining her social autonomy in relation to the others in the group of terrorists. But also it increases her autonomy in contrast to what it was in her status as prisoner of war. With her new role, the nature of her relationship has changed because she is no longer the reluctant captive. Accordingly, the coerciveness of the relationship is affected, we postulate, in one of two ways: either (1) she is wholly dominated by the group and loses all her social autonomy as a separate rational being; or else (2) she acquires a new independence. In either case, the group loses its coercive hold over the victim and replaces it with a different 'role' relationship.

In the first instance Y becomes or is reduced to being an instrument of the group's ideological warfare, much as slaves are as mere tools to their masters or as members of certain notorious religious cults are as brainwashed agents of their leadership. The methods used by the group to 'instrumentalize' its victim may, of course, be coercive (e.g., scarce feedings, punishment-reward tactics, forced sleeplessness, isolation and beatings and threats of beatings, "good-guy-bad-guy" tactics, and other control techniques). These are designed to alter the victim's attitude and so her motives and actions. The eventual outcome is the formation of a different role relationship between Y and her erstwhile captors. In her new role, Y has a different type and range of autonomy which the group controls: it is a noncoercive form of control, which the group exerts upon all its members as such. Y's new role affords an autonomy unlike what she had when she was independent from the group prior to the abduction. That autonomy has been erased, along with the coercion that had diminished it. Her new autonomy, as it relates to the new role, is virtually a function of being an agent of the ideological program of the terrorists. She has been coerced into her status of 'instrument', but the success of the methods of terror is shown by X's being able to control Y noncoercively.

In the second instance Y, the victim, accepts the 'education' she has been subjected to and adopts the 'situation' of the group. She makes the group's aims her aims as she comes to view things its way. In other words, she internalizes the identity of the group, and this forms the core of her new role relation to the others in the group of terrorists. In making common cause with the group, the former coercive relationship has been transformed into one of 'fellow revolutionary warrior'. As she carries out her new role, her increasing autonomy in that role marks the decreasing coercion to which she is subject in her relation to the group. In a sense, personal 'choice' plays some part also because she rejects the role of victim and replaces it with a partnership role in the group's ideological program.

The first diagram (1) depicts the success the terrorist group X (through agency of X^1 as well) has in "winning over" Y, inspite of her continuing desire to escape. She has gradually altered her attitude and feelings and her 'will' and behavior towards X. Accordingly, she transforms her part in the role her captors have cast for her, namely, from unwilling and fearful victim to the acquiescing, increasingly cooperative victim who can now be persuaded without recourse to threats, abuse, and violence to do or refrain from doing whatever finite tasks her captors dictate or expect. On the other hand, in the second diagram, Y loses all autonomy and becomes an instrument of S.

PHASE 4

This final phase in our analytical scheme occurs as she, Y, develops a sense of identification between herself and the group, X. At this point, which is an almost imperceptible development from Phase 3, Y no longer manifests the desire to, or even seeks to, escape, since she now belongs to the group as a full-fledged member. Indeed, Y openly and publicly proclaims her new role relation in both word and deed.

A very fine line is crossed by Y between being a collaborator whose 'consent' has been coerced and one whose consent is uncoerced. Suppose the victim accepted the role of urban revolutionary in exchange for her life or had been 'brainwashed' into assuming this role. Her role change, whatever her motivation, lessens and perhaps eliminates X's coercive control over Y and y. But how important 'motive' is to be considered in *justifying* Y's new role is a separate matter from the coerciveness of her relationship, that is, whether Y is blamed or excused for her behaviors in relation to X.

REVIEW

My basic claim has been to show that various changing roles between participants may affect both the nature of the relationship and its coerciveness. That is, as certain roles change, the dynamic relationship may become more, less, or not coercive, despite that the participants, actions, and context remain substantially the same. This is what I mean by coercion as a dynamic relational concept. In addition, as the context of coercion and the relationship change, the relative autonomy of each participant shifts and with it the balance of power between them, particularly an unwanted diminishment of the victim's autonomy because of the respective role relationships.

In Phase 1 the victim's behavior is reactive, submissive, and capitulatory because it is premised both on fear and a desire to escape. She has lost her former autonomy and has very little, if any, social autonomy with respect to her captors. The terrorist band that abducted her played no role in any of her relationships prior to the abduction. On the terrorists' side of things, on the contrary, she was cast in a role by its members: she was the 'means' by which they expected to achieve certain political goals or advance their revolutionary aims. Their 'role' with respect to their victim is of a band of militant revolutionaries engaged in armed struggle against a contested power, their captive being an important pawn in their strategy. This role, together with its expectations, aims, tactics, and so on, influences the coercer's behavior in relation to the victim and explains the initial outcome: the imposition of a new role upon the victim and an enlargement of the coercer's autonomy *at the expense* of the victim.

Their respective roles heavily influence their interactions. For instance, the early role as victim-abductee-captive is a key element in explaining her relationship to the band and not merely the various actions she may perform in response to her captors, regardless of whether the actions are sometimes motivated by fear for her personal safety or a reluctance to do anything or whether they are sometimes voluntary. Only in the case of fear is her behavior unequivocally coerced, but we insist that all her behaviors occur within the role relationship forcibly established and generally maintained.

As the relationship between the participants is transformed, it is because the roles are changed; the dynamic and relative spheres of autonomy of the participant are altered and redefined, and so are the behaviors influenced by them. Conversely, the changing behaviors contribute in turn to the 'role' changes taking place.

In the succeeding phases a new set of role behaviors and attitudes seem to intersect and eventually displace the previous ones. For instance, an attitude on the victim's part gradually shifts from resistance modes to coexistence and accommodation to her abductors. Consequently, the role she comes to assume means a lessening of her role status as 'coerced victim' and more a standing of 'cooperative captive', and so on. Hence, the overall relationship retains its coerciveness to some extent despite that the interactions become less overtly coercive (and more conciliatory).

Finally, the eventual role assumed by the erstwhile 'victim' becomes one of ostensible collaborator, activist, and sympathizer.

To the degree she has been 'brainwashed' (as a result of the deliberate use of 'control' techniques), she is not regarded as a person with any reasonable amount of self-control and accountability over her actions because, as these techniques succeed, the subjective motives and intentions behind the victim's behavior are not her own but rather those her controllers wish her to have, in spite of the fact that the mere possession of them influences the behavior of the possessor. The 'brainwashed' victim's behavior is an instrument of the controller.

On the other hand, as the 'victim' collaborates with and actively seeks to advance the 'cause' of the terrorist band, the social role used to describe her relationship with its members no longer describes her behavioral interaction, for she assumes another sort of role heavily influencing her conduct, namely, being a participating, co-equal member of the group. As the roles of the group change, the relationship becomes less and less coercive, and her behavior is no longer coerced.

essential ECs

P ──────→ p
Q ──────→ q

Where P is the coercer, Q is the coercee, p is the instrumental action, and q is the coerced behavior.

will

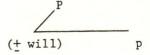

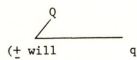

consent

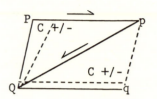

Where P is the coercer, Q is the coercee, p is the instrument of coercion, q is the target behavior for coercion, and C +/− is an action (not) consented to by Q in response to P or P's doing p.

choice

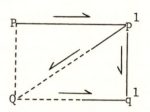

Where ____ is the control P, Q has over doing p, q respectively, and ____ . . . ____ is the degree of control a participant has over his or her own action (Q retains some minimal choice over doing q).

intentions/motives

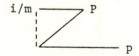   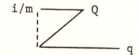

Where i/m indicates there is an intention/motive for P or Q that may (not) be executed.

want, needs, wishes, desires

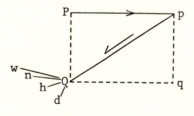

Where n/w/h/d indicates there is a need, want, wish, or desire for participants P, Q within the class of wilfull action (qualification: although n/w/h/d may define P's role and explain his or her behavior, it is mainly Q's n/w/h/d that is central to P's coerciveness (when n/w/h/d are central to a definition of coercion).

EXAMPLE II: CUBAN MISSILE CRISIS

THE FACTS

In what has since been dubbed the Cuban Missile Crisis, a serious confrontation between the two nuclear superpowers, the United States of America and the USSR, it has become clear to American intelligence agents that an important military change had occurred on the island of Communist Cuba. The Soviet leadership had begun to deploy offensive (and no longer simply defensive) weaponry—including nuclear missiles—on the soil of its client state, Cuba, and had commenced large-scale construction of installations from which this weaponry could be used (presumably against the United States, less than 100 miles from the Cuban shore).

The American response came swiftly and contributed to the inevitable escalation of 'confrontational' events. Among other steps taken by President John F. Kennedy, a quarantine was put in place consisting of a naval blockade that would turn back all ships bound for Cuba carrying offensive military cargo. Then, an American spy-plane was shot down over Cuban airspace.

Tensions heightened between the two powers, bringing humankind to the brink of nuclear war. President Kennedy and the Soviet leader, Chairman Nikita Khrushchev, exchanged a series of letters containing American demands and Soviet responses. As the situation reached the point of critical confrontation, the Soviet leader sent a message to Kennedy stating that the Soviet government had ordered the immediate dismantling of the (offensive) launch sites and the removal of all nuclear missiles and bases from Cuban territory. It also ordered its ships not to proceed towards the blockade.

It was Robert S. McNamara (Kennedy's Secretary of Defense) who said that the American "objective was to force the missiles out of Cuba without war."[1] The objective was to be reached by a strategy of increased pressure against the Soviets.

British Prime Minister Harold Macmillan described the resolution of the crisis as follows: "The crisis was short, it lasted from October 16, when irrefutable evidence became known in Washington of the Russian deployment of nuclear missiles in Cuba, till

October 28, when the news came of Khrushchev's compliance with American demands.''[2]

THE PROBLEM

Such descriptions of historically momentous events suggest a classic case of coercion. Khrushchev was compelled against his will to yield to Kennedy's demands due to sufficient pressure being brought by the latter against the former.

On the other hand, Robert Kennedy (the President's brother and Attorney General) presented a different approach to the same set of facts when he described it as an agreement between two parties wherein Khrushchev made an "offer"[3] to withdraw offensive weapons systems from Cuba if the United States would agree not to invade Cuba. President Kennedy responded by accepting Khrushchev's "offer." What followed, then, was Soviet compliance with the terms of the agreement.

In this view of the exchanges, coercion is not the likely label to pin on this relationship. One merely suggesting it as being an execution of the terms of an agreement seems more appropriate.

Whether or not coercion aptly describes the Kennedy-Khrushchev relationship is not our chief concern; what is, however, is an account of the factors that would help us make the best judgment. If the Soviet leader was indeed coerced by Kennedy, a significant factor at play in the coerciveness of the relationship is the social role each assumed in relation to the other. Thus, our analysis and judgment is deficient or off the mark if we use only the following as our criterion: the mere bending of one party's will to the design imposed (or methods applied) by the 'coercing' will of the other party.

ANALYSIS

Several factors relating to the participants and their relationship should be properly accounted for prior to a determination of coercion.

The two leaders were, of course, individual persons whose private wills, preferences, motives, choices, needs, wishes, and expectations had their customary crucial influence upon their interactions. Accordingly, if our analysis is to apply within this limited framework of subjective mind-states or mind-events, it becomes readily apparent how Macmillan could claim that Khrushchev yielded or was coerced into complying with Kennedy's demands or threats, that is, to eschew both increasingly unendurable American pressure and the likely result, nuclear war.

In this view the participants are regarded as isolated individuals between whom the various intervening variables contributing to their final decisions *in relation to each other* are of secondary, or even no, relevant importance. Such variables as political or official agency, national interest, military preparedness and capability, intelligence access, flow of information control, personality profile of adversary, and so on, receive little or no attention in an argument claiming that certain coercive instruments ('pressure' in the form of serious threats such as high military alert status, unusual troop movement, and so forth) are used by one party (Kennedy) to control coercively the actions of the other party (Khrushchev).

This approach underplays the key factor (or 'role') of political agency because both Kennedy and Khrushchev are official political figures at the leadership of their respective countries and as such do not act merely as individuals. When they act as officials, they do so as agents, and not merely as private persons. Hence it is not quite accurate to portray the resolution of this crisis as if 'the will' of one party was purposefully bent merely in concession to 'the will' of the other party.

Instead, the *role* of each participant in relation to the other should be considered as being the more basic, influential factor in causing the outcome. 'Role' most closely reflects the multiplicity of factors defining whether or not this truly was an act or relationship of coercion between Kennedy and Khrushchev. Any coercive relationship that may have existed between the two leaders was due mainly to the relative power, resources, intelligence, and determination at the command of each with regards to the other. It should not be considered as simply the one's personal capitulation to the will of the other. Further, their respective roles, in relation to each other, define their relative autonomy in the relationship and, hence, the degree of control one participant can exercise over the other at any one time.

RATIONALE FOR THE 'ROLE' APPROACH

Indeed, neither Kennedy nor Khrushchev could act alone as private persons in their *social* (i.e., political, legal, and so on) positions as President and Chairman (though at times during the ordeal it must have seemed to the participants that it was, in the end, one's lone will pitted against the will of the other). For these give to their holders certain powers as well as bring them into certain types of (role) relations with others that they would otherwise not possess. Therefore, they act *in terms of* their positions, which is, of course, not to deny the impact of their personal tastes, wishes, intelligence, preferences, and so on, on their official decisions and actions.

It is probably a truism that the more autocratic or tyrannical a ruler is, the more play is given in decisions to his or her personal whims because there exist fewer constraints upon the ruler's behavior. Kennedy and Khrushchev did have crucial official constraints on their behavior, such as the condition of being of demonstrable 'sound mind' (at least to their own colleagues). On the other hand, it is certainly conceivable for rational people using reasonable 'means', to reach ultimately irrational conclusions, but a broader context of factors would come into play than the limited ones considered in their calculations, for example, political survival, national interest, and so forth. Hence, the advice and pressures the leaders receive (or are subjected to) through their advisors, the control of information flow to them, and their legal-political power to command or initiate military/political actions on behalf of their own countries with or without consultation from other official segments of the government (e.g., Congress, the Politbureau) all serve to influence in crucially important ways the interactions and interrelationship between the two leaders.

THE SOLUTION: COERCION AND ROLE
IN OUR EXAMPLE

The claim that Khrushchev simply complied with American (i.e., Kennedy's) demands is, in the foregoing analysis, a misleading oversimplification. But so is the other (McNamara's) claim that, by implication, Khrushchev was forced to yield to the pressure *simpliciter* applied by Kennedy.

It may be that it was not a capitulation to pressure that was crucial in causing Khrushchev to do what he did, but perhaps it was the Soviet leadership's strongest desire to avoid the price it undoubtedly would pay in a military confrontation. Yet, even if this were so, this interaction might still be coercive since Khrushchev's options were being determined not by him but by the Americans. The Americans constrained the Soviets to act as they did in avoiding the confrontation *but only because* the Soviets valued the avoidance of nuclear war (at that time). Thus, it would not be a clear-cut case of coercion because the Americans did not control the 'value' that presumably was most highly prized and so, given the available alternatives, caused the Soviet withdrawal.

More to the point, the Soviet government responded as it did in avoiding a military show-down through its most visible aspect, its leader. Even if Khrushchev ordinarily was instrumental in framing Soviet policy as well as in influencing its practice during the Crisis, his decisions were not merely or primarily his own but were state decisions. His own personal will at times may have been indistinguishable from his political will (namely, the personal impetus to make, take, and execute political decisions on behalf of his nation's immediate interests). So, in a particular *political* (and not personal) relationship like the one in which he was engaged with Kennedy, each participant is a political agent who more or less carries into effect or has carried into effect the political will and judgment of the political entity he expresses or represents.

A (human) political agent may or may not choose to execute his or her own will or that of the collective to which he or she belongs. It is, therefore, not accurate to suppose that the decisions he or she makes or actions he or she orders others to take occur simply in relation to other personalities/individuals alone as though they are interacting immediately (i.e., without mediation), mutually influencing, or causing their actions, reactions, and interactions.

Whether Kennedy coerced Khrushchev in this affair must be established on the basis (besides factoring in the flurry of memoranda passed between the principals which likely contributed to the appearance that only two individuals were involved and were merely responding to each other's wishes, motives, desires, and so on) of the social roles of each of the participants, in terms of which their relations with each other were structured and their mutual interactions conducted.

The inclusion and convergence of all these other factors should make it obvious that Khrushchev was *not* merely coerced by Kennedy into withdrawing the missiles from Cuba and turning the Soviet ships around before a clash occurred over the naval blockade. Neither is it correct to claim that Khrushchev acted autonomously and with full freedom or independence of Kennedy in reaching the decision he did.

It probably is most fair to state that a number of factors influenced the final decision of the Soviet leader, some of which he and the other leaders in the Kremlin were forcibly confronted with by the Americans. It was thoroughly inimical to what he and the Soviet government would have desired. Thus, in deciding whether this was a case of coercion, it would depend upon the actual *degree* to which the American government not only controlled the behavior of the Soviet decision-making process but actually caused the Soviets (through their agent, Khrushchev) to do what they did.

It is not necessary (though perhaps interesting, nevertheless) to make a precise determination about coercion in this case because my sole purpose in introducing the Cuban Missile Crisis has been to show that *role relations* are a decidedly crucial factor, especially in political relationships (since these are essentially role-structured), in this type of context. The diplomacy between two powerful nations may evolve, under certain circumstances, into a new dimension involving the leaders in ways that make an 'interpersonal' approach to their relationship more appropriate because they interact more as 'powerful' individuals than as leaders of powerful states. But this consideration should not obscure the basically political (i.e., role) nature and consequences of 'personal' diplomacy. In addition, social role also functions in interpersonal relations, and this, too, will have to be considered when judging that coercion (had not) occurred.

In the Missile Crisis example the basic social roles of the two principal participants remained generally unchanged, though the autonomy of Khrushchev was affected by Kennedy. Once we recognize that 'role' does figure in the mutual influence one participant has upon the other, it becomes clear that the nature of their evolving relationship during the Crisis is not so simply described, as Macmillan and others have done, as one party using certain instruments to influence and control the other.

Macmillan's phrase "compliance with American demands" does indeed suggest coercion in its classic form, namely, the coercer is a party who, after applying certain measures against another party (the coercee), causes that party to do (or refrain from doing) something the coercee would ordinarily not choose to do in the absence of those measures. In this sense, then, Kennedy issues demands and applies pressure, leaving Khrushchev no choice but to submit. The utter simplicity of this formulation, however, belies the complexity of the interactive relationship between the participants because, in the main, it overlooks the 'role' factor in its various intricacies.

In general, the objectionable thing about coercion is its infringement upon social autonomy. In the case of the Missile Crisis, the *roles* of these 'political' participants predefined the shifting and changing realm of social autonomy each has in relation to the other, the consequence being that coercive control, if it had occurred, could have been exercised only with respect to the deliberate limitations imposed on autonomy, since each interacted with the other not as an individual, but as a political agent, as a chief of state. Such roles as these are highly complex networks of international and domestic power, authority, resources, reactions. Changes in any of these aspects do not always alter the role itself.

If autonomy is role-defined, how is it that autonomy may change while role remains the same? The range of social autonomy is most usually pre-set by the type of role engaging the parties, though it is also the case that roles may become replaced by other roles as the relative autonomy of participants shifts, i.e., roles may change in influence, priority, nature, and so on. Factors contributing, on the other hand, to 'autonomy shifts' may include role changes themselves, changes in fortune and resources of participants, circumstances, and so on. Thus, social autonomy, while still being role-dependent, may become altered in degree despite the unchanged overall nature of the participants' roles only because certain aspects of their roles change in what is normally understood to be a complex of features associated with certain roles (e.g., like heads of state). Accordingly, the role of Soviet leader, clearly one of powerful political agency, remains the same in general, although, for example, certain of its critics from within the government may be silenced for one reason or another. In effect, this increases social autonomy and decision-making power for the leader, and yet the nature of the role connected with such autonomy persists in relation to the Americans.

In summary, the role relationship between the two leaders remained generally the same, but through the measures he took and the demand he made on behalf of the American government, Kennedy had altered to some extent Khrushchev's range of social autonomy. Thus, Khrushchev and the Soviets were compelled to avoid a military confrontation. It was not Khrushchev's personal autonomy nor his will that the Americans infringed upon, as it was certainly not coercion in the usual sense that occurred. Rather, it was his loss of social autonomy as a political (role-defined) agent that suffered because of the American actions. In this view, some degree of coercion occurred but only in the limited sense that the only option Kennedy closed for the Soviets was the attempt to run the blockade with either expendable risk or impunity. Owing to the Soviet (leader's) obvious priority on the absolute undersirability of nuclear war at that time, the decision to avoid a show-down was made.

Thus, it is possible to argue either way, namely, that Khrushchev was not coerced because he sought to pursue a course that would avoid war, and this is what he did. On the other hand, he may have been coerced because the Americans controlled (by constraint) the option he ultimately took. In any case, this is no clear-cut instance of coercion. Khrushchev was not *personally* coerced since it was in virtue of his social role as leader that he was implicated in the affair. He could have chosen to resign his position, a viable alternative not controlled by the Americans, thereby releasing him from any American control upon his personal autonomy. But since it was his social autonomy as a political leader in relation to the Americans that was at stake, that is, the Soviet government was constrained not to run the blockade because of the imponderable risk it faced in doing so, the Soviets were coerced *only to the extent* that what they ultimately did was caused by the American actions. Of course, the ambiguity surrounding 'coercion' is, in this case, attributable to a deficiency in real knowledge about Soviet decision-making and not to the term itself.

If, in this affair, the Soviet government did indeed forfeit some of its autonomy in relation to the Americans because of what the latter had done, it is the role the Soviet leader played that determined both the nature of his social autonomy and its range as a result of the American actions.

NOTES

1. Robert Kennedy, *Thirteen Days* (New York: W. W. Norton, 1969), p. 15.
2. Ibid., p. 18.
3. Ibid., pp. 102-4, 110.

CHAPTER 6

Coercion and the Influence of Ideology

THE MEANING OF COERCION

Etymology

The general and root meaning of coercion, as we in the West understand it, is *coercere,* Latin for "to surround." It is more remotely originated from two other Latin words, *arca* ("box," "coffin") and *arcere* ("to shut in"). Coercion, like other terms with similar beginnings, signifies, in very broad terms, certain spatial characteristics of human existence, all denoting some type of 'spatial' restraint.[1] Being deliberately physically prevented from using one's 'physical' space is only a single form of coercion, others being 'nonphysical' restraints on one's 'inner' space.

However, unless we understand 'space' in the present contextual analysis as a metaphor, we will not be able to make sense of 'coercion' in its variety of instances, for example, in those involving the 'inner space' of (not) being able to make choices, a key feature of human autonomy.

In this broad, metaphorical sense, both 'coercion' and 'autonomy' indicate the participants' ability to control their own space *relative to each other.* In particular, social role, as we have suggested, in part defines the participant's relative range and use of space (i.e., concerning choices, effective actions, and relationships).

Ideology

Another important influence on the meaning and use of 'coercion', in addition to etymology, is ideology. Ideological considerations have affected not only questions concerning the justifiability of coercion but mainly the manner in which coercion is conceived, though this is not at all obvious to the casual observer. The concept of coercion must be seen as having a history correlative to some great degree with the 'historical' meanings of autonomy.

Coercion belongs to a subclass of social control relations. Any claim one makes to a coercively controlled abridgment of a subject-participant's social autonomy depends, conceptually, upon the range of autonomy initially predicated of the coercee-participant. The coercee's social autonomy diminishes because the autonomy of the coercer increases due to the coercer's use of a control technique at the victim's expense.

The way in which ideologies have defined the social autonomy (or its range) of the coercer-coercee can best be seen in their sometimes subtle conceptualization of the human person (i.e., the subject-participant). Thus, social relations between abstractly conceived individuals might be expected to differ conceptually from relations between intrinsically social or community ideas of human persons. For this reason, 'social autonomy' is also conceived differently. Our focus will now be on the relational aspect of coercion because the relative and shifting spheres of autonomy are conceived as correlative with the idea of personhood.

In general, contemporary views of coercion are framed to some extent on the basis of the dominant ideologies of modern individualism and nonindividualism. Of course, this claim is not meant to deny that coercion and other violations against humanity were unknown or nonexistent in ancient society or in societies radically different from our own. Instead it means that the human person and his or her relationship to his or her community were conceived differently, which in turn has influenced how coercion and social autonomy are seen.

That this claim should not be surprising is due to the teaching of modern cultural philosophy and anthropology which has shown that, as background to our claim, each culture holds a set of implicit beliefs about society and the natural world as well as about the perception that forges experience. Thus, in unique cultures, the experiences of their peoples differ. Perhaps this also implies that, to some degree, human consciousness is a social formation.

In any case, an example of the contrast between two different cultures is found in the modern notion of individual moral autonomy with its origins in the European Enlightenment and ancient Judaism's rejection of any pretension that a person might do "that which was right in his own eyes" (Judges 17:6). Even today there are various 'nonindividualist' cultures which, like the Chinese, have difficulty conceptualizing an individual 'self' completely detached from society's values.[2] Indeed, it is now commonly acknowledged that it is a distinctive notion of modern Western cultural philosophy that comprehends the self as being so separate from its social and natural environment.

In other words, if human autonomy likewise receives a variety of historical-philosophical meanings, no univocal and transhistorical significance exists for coercion and other similar violations of 'human autonomy'.

We shall now discuss some ideas about selfhood, autonomy, and coercion drawn from selected philosophers and different periods or traditions of philosophy in history. It is a basic claim of this work that a general correlation exists between coercion and ideology.

THE IDEOLOGICAL BACKGROUND OF COERCION

By the term 'ideology' I refer to the comprehensive system of beliefs about defining and interpreting social and political reality with respect to the means, goals, and values required either to reproduce or perfect the reality so conceived. Accordingly, some views of personhood, autonomy, and coercion and social relations have an 'ideological' character, but not because they misrepresent reality (as is ordinarily presumed in calling something 'ideological'). Some social 'facts' themselves (e.g., the 'atomic individual' of Classical Liberalism) are such only because of the social theories and the ideology behind them in which their believers perceive them.

A pithy survey of both traditional and contemporary views should demonstrate the correlation we discern in the influence of ideology upon the conception of coercion. Hence, our chief focus will be political and not merely interpersonal social relations.

Israelites

In the ancient society of the Israelites, there is evidence of very little self-conscious individuality. The group's identity was at the center of a person's self-identity. The explanation and justification of actions and social relations between group members were determined by specific myths, norms, beliefs, and rules governing social life.

The social autonomy possessed by individual group members was construed in terms of membership *in* and not against or from the group. Thus, a coercive relationship between members and tribal authorities meant not abridgments of individual autonomy but rather personal gain at the expense of the group's cohesion and, perhaps as well, a transgression of divine precepts (sure to bring disfavor upon the group's destiny).[3] Tribal authorities were not seen as independent political entities.

For ancient groups like these, the subjectivism and modern idea of personal privacy usually associated with the 'natural' autonomy of the individual were typically nonexistent. "The primitive trait of privacy . . . meant literally a state of being deprived of something, even of the highest and most human of man's capacities. A person who lived only a private life, who like the slave was not permitted to enter the public realm, or like the barbarian, had chosen not to establish such a realm, was not fully human." Furthermore, a life spent outside the public realm, in the privacy of 'one's own' (*idion*) is 'idiotic' by definition.[4] ('Solitude' should not be equated here with the ideological notion of 'privacy').

Ancient Greeks

In contrast to the ancient semitic society, the Greek outlook was more individualized because it was rooted in the idea of the state and in a concept of the individual citizen's relation to political order. The writings of Plato and Aristotle are representative as expressions of the self-concept of Classical Greece.

The metaphysics of the human soul give the Greek philosophers their basis for an analysis and understanding of human life. It is based on a vision of a natural, rational balance existing between the various parts of the soul. Each part is to assume its 'natural' place and function and thus is to be accorded its proper due. This is its 'good'. 'The good' is the same for both the individual and the state. Nevertheless, 'the good' of the state is held to be the more perfect good because it is a higher, if not separate and distinct, part of the soul of life.

To alter one's fixed place in nature provokes disharmony and imbalance. As the individual's soul could become enslaved by the unnatural domination of the intellectual by the passionate parts, so, too, political states could be impelled by pure desire to do things against their intelligent will, ending in disharmony (e.g., fear and poverty.) Hence, the Greek philosophers believed that there are natural relations of control and domination (and therefore, of autonomy) in the process of self-realization.

In the context of these ideals, coercion may be understood in terms of the usurpation of human rational self-control. Mastery over one's own soul is essential to the achievement of self-realization. Even social control (and particularly coercion) is seen as a type of 'self-control', the 'self' being continuous with the individual and the state. The essence of coercion lies in the disharmony provoked by causing the victim to do or forbear something against his or her *informed* or rational consent because it is contrary to nature.[5]

The stress in Greek philosophy on the rationality of natural relations is illustrated in Aristotle's view of slavery. Slavery is held to be a natural condition of total servitude where a slave's place is fixed by nature in his or her relations to others. It signifies absolute domination and control by others. The slave, like the uneducable person, is bereft of a citizen's birthright as well as a rational capacity to master his or her own affairs. Thus, Aristotle belives, some external compulsion is required for his or her own, and society's, good ('self-realization'). It is needed to promote the social function of slavery.

Analogously, noncoercive force may be deliberately applied by a scribe to his or her pen as he or she strives towards realizing him or herself as a writer and towards utilizing the pen's 'natural' function as a writing tool. Likewise, compulsion against slaves—to use a most dramatic example—is required, but it is noncoercive because the soul of a slave is properly realized when its corresponding activity of being a slave is enforced. Neither the slave nor the citizen has a personal or social autonomy apart from the essentials of his or her soul. Consequently, the use of force to establish or promote 'the good' is noncoercive. On the other hand, the autonomy of a citizen, born of officially recognized rights, duties, and privileges, would be contrary to the natural order of things if given to a slave. Enslavement is both fixed and noncoercive (of course, modern

Western democracies reject in principle the idea that a person's place in society is preestablished by nature).

STOICISM

The Greek and Roman philosophies of stoicism added a new dimension to the concept of personhood in the Platonic-Aristotelian tradition: the universal equality of all rational beings. It is from the standpoint of 'natural law' that this philosophy proclaimed a certain individual autonomy between persons owing to their equal status as rational human beings.[6]

Thomas Aquinas (1224-1274)

However, individualism in its modern usage begins to emerge in the medieval philosophy of Thomas Aquinas where the individual is conceived abstractly as a moral finality and is to be treated as such by all fellow rational beings.

The autonomy of individual conscience is, for Aquinas, the result of the participation of divine law in rational creatures. This, coupled with his advocacy of the general principle that "every man must act in consonance with reason" shows that Aquinas' philosophy is a progressive development in the conception of individualism as it begins to assert the autonomy of the individual in the moral realm. In general, the medieval religious idea of individualism is that all persons are children of God, and so, before God, all are equal.

Aquinas intimates that any interference by others in the expressive acts of will of any individual is, because it originates in a source exterior to the individual, to be regarded as unnatural and against the design or purpose of nature.[7] His rationalistic analysis of existence and human action continues to conceive of personhood abstractly as the possessor of reason and as subject to natural laws whose objective norms must be known and are a precondition to self-realization.

Coercion, therefore, is no longer understood in terms of the elements of group or mythic solidarity or the elements of rational soul, but it is defined with respect to the existential actions as expression of the autonomy of human will, guided by the objective norms of the laws of nature originating from God.

The Modern Contractarians

Thomas Hobbes (1588-1679), John Locke (1632-1704), and Jean Jacques Rousseau (1712-1778) are joined as contractarians in the sense that each gives a secularistic, individualistic variation on a theory of consent as the basis of government and civil society.

Hobbes' political theory is a case for political absolutism, meaning the virtual supremacy of the state over the individual. It is the ruler, not the subject, who is sovereign. The sovereign political body ("Leviathan") is said to be instituted by means of a tacit consent of each individual party to the putative covenant. Not being itself a party to the contract, the sovereign is, by its very nature, not constrained by its terms. Nor is it merely an authoritative body to prevent 'incorrigible egoism'. The sovereign's virtually unlimited power, Hobbes argues, gives the individual subject his liberty and social autonomy.

In convenanting with others to establish a sovereign for mutual protection, natural persons alienate their natural powers or rights to the sovereign to whom has been vouchsafed the responsibility for safeguarding the convenantors: "Whatsoever is done to a man, conformable to his own will signified to the doer, is no injury to him."[8] If coercion is a form of injury to the victim because it denies his or her will, the covenantors have, by their consent, legitimated the sovereign's power to do what it will in the interest of the commonwealth. The paradoxical consequence of Hobbes' ideological conception of life in civil society is that the subjects' autonomy is defined by the necessities of sovereign power, which thereby makes a subject's independent will nullified or overruled by the superior will of the sovereign preestablished by the subject's consent.

John Locke, like Hobbes, claims that human society begins when individuals chose to place themselves under political rule in order to protect their property and to escape the instability and rapacity of life in a state of nature.[9] Government is instituted to preserve the natural rights of individuals. Unlike Hobbes, it is Locke's belief in natural rights that predetermines the sovereign's spheres of individual autonomy with regards to the government. For Hobbes, only the political entity is sovereign, whereas for Locke, all political authority ultimately derives from the conception of the sovereign individual. Natural rights define the social autonomy of individual citizens in Locke's ideology of the human person. Coercion has now become a much more individual matter.

Jean Jacques Rousseau also identifies freedom and autonomy with government by consent, but he equates 'consent' with participation in the general will of society and not with representation in government, as Locke's theory has done.

In Rousseau's political theory, it is the metaphysical "General Will" that ultimately determines human autonomy because it displaces the individual's private conscience as a guide in public affairs. Hence, coercive abridgments of autonomy in Rousseau's conception of civil society would be reckoned differently than they would be in conscience- or rights-based, control-based, or divine concepts of society.

The 'general will' is the artificial product of natural persons ('noble savages') who voluntarily merge to form society. Its formative basis is the rational set of interests that all individual members of society possess. The creator of justice and morality is the 'general will' not God nor nature. It is the social contract that produced a moral, collective body from which originates the individual members' social rights, as well as their obligations to submit to the 'general will'.

Because it is believed to embody the basic common interests of all members of society, the 'general will' is more important that any private interest or aggregate of such interests. The protection of common interests forms the contractual justification for the existence of organized society. As Rousseau states, "the particular will naturally tends to preferences, and the general will to equality."[10]

Society is not conceived, as with the other contract theorists, as distinct from its associate members but only from the *private* interests of its members. The "social individual" in Rousseau's philosophy is not a self-sufficient person with only private and subjective features whose "inner" integrity society must preserve. It is the public set of features that has social priority. Accordingly, it is the individual's autonomy that is defined in terms of obedience to, and not independence from, society's laws and its 'general will'.

Immanuel Kant (1724-1804)

In Kant's philosophy is the view of a good society as a totality of law-governed social relations, reflecting the unique metaphysical status of human individuality as seen 'in the light of reason'. Kant construes as a universal command of reason that a rational being should always act so as to treat humanity, whether in his own person or in that of any other, as an end in itself, never merely as a means.

This unique moral quality of human individuality is basic to Kant's concept of society, which he considers a "union of different rational beings in a system of common laws." He calls this ideal union a *kingdom of ends.*

Kant acknowledges that his ideal society depends upon his concept of a rational creature being one who constructs universal laws by a rational assertion of will but who also is subject to the universal laws thus created. The legitimate obligatoriness of a moral system of laws derives from the postulate that laws must originate from the actions of those who are subjected to them. Therefore, he holds that every single person in society has the supreme duty to obey universally valid laws. To enforce this duty "lawful public coercion is necessary to enforce the abstract demands of reason and justice, and so overcome the natural antagonisms of egoism in human nature."

From his concept of a rational being he derives several a priori social-moral principles: (1) the *"freedom* of every member of society *as a human being"*; (2) the *"equality* of each with all the others as a *subject"*; and (3) the *"independence* of each member of a commonwealth *as a citizen."*[11] It is important that Kant's theory of abstract, rational individualism forms the basis for a notion of human social autonomy.

In society the autonomy of each rational being is defined by the self-willed actions that embody a universal rational principle. Since, for Kant, a "free will" and a "free will subject to moral law" are the same thing, the key rationalistic element in his view of coercion is not whether the will's 'freedom' is restricted per se but whether it is restrictively controlled by another's will when it is grounded on universal law.

The latter speaks to the justification for coercion, while the former is simply the basis for it. In any case, the rational moral autonomy of an abstractly conceived, relationless individual in society is a once-and-for-all, fixed dimension of personhood, the same for all persons. Contemporary Western views of human

autonomy and coercion owe much to Kant's theory of individualism, particularly as expressed by philosophies that claim coercion
on the basis of an infringement upon the abstract individuality of a
person virtually regardless of context, since a person's social-moral
autonomy remains the same.

G.W.F. Hegel (1770-1831)

Hegel's philosophy in general is an important reaction against
the abstract individualism of the Enlightenment (e.g., in Hobbes,
Locke, Rousseau, and Kant). It was also opposed to classical
liberalism because it failed to acknowledge the basic social nature
of an individual's personality. It portrayed civil society and the
state mistakenly as external and fortuitous to human personality
and moral development.

For Hegel, the true 'personhood' of a human being is possible
only to the degree that he relinquishes his claim to private
uniqueness. He must permit himself to be considered a facet of the
social totality to which he belongs. Hegel claims that it is existence
of the state that makes possible a rational and free existence for its
citizens.

When Hegel mentions the freedom of an individual's will, he
means at least human freedom in the earliest stage of the will's
development where the will is purely arbitrary because it is
dominated by impulses and inclinations. But he also means the
condition of a higher ethical maturity of the will where human
freedom achieves the essence of a rational will. The rational will is
free because it has its existence in the rational community.

Hegel's view is distinguished from Rousseau's and Kant's, for
they conceive of a 'general will' of a state as being the common
good that grows from the particular individual will, the point at
which their political analysis begins. Hegel, on the other hand,
conceives of the common good solely as the "absolutely rational
part of the will."

In Hegel's idealistic metaphysics, 'reason' is the ultimate
grounding of the universe and is manifested in the rationality of the
will and in the organic unity of the state. Human beings are at the
service of reason. Under its direction they establish the institutions
of state which Hegel believes are the outward (external) and highest

expressions of the evolving realization of reason. In brief, Hegel's idea of the state rests on 'reason', not force. He was opposed to the view that when freedom is meant as the freedom to pursue selfish desires and satisfactions, social existence is possible only if external constraints are forcefully imposed on this freedom. Government is then seen as an external agent of force to meet the social necessities of life.

Hegel makes the interesting claim that "there is no coercion;" no person "has ever been coerced or ever will be." He argues that coercion is, in a sense, impossible among rational beings because when reason exists in a person as his or her will, the inner conviction of the rational will is beyond the reach of all external (coercing) forces. Hegel's individualism restricts 'freedom' to a purely inward meaning. A free will cannot be coerced at all unless it continues to (1) hold its idea of possession of the external object as one's free essence; or (2) grasp the object itself.

In itself "coercion is nothing real" since human freedom is absolute. Though external force may be applied, imposing the will of an alien power upon a free being, Hegel says that the victim is subdued, never coerced,[12] since a free rational being can always choose death rather than capitulate to attempted coercion, the will remains absolutely free.

Karl Marx (1818-1883)

In his philosophy, Marx held that in a class-dominated society inter-class relations are defined by domination, exploitation, and irreconcilable antagonism. Hence, any pretense of *human* autonomy and freedom is distorted, perpetuation of property interests leads to brutal conflicts, and the self-fulfillment of human personality is thwarted. In Marx's view these antagonisms will vanish with the total elimination of classes, so that the resultant classless society is the primary objective social condition for human self-fulfillment.[13] Marx's philosophy is mainly a critique of existing (capitalist) society.

In general Marx rejected the claim that society is nothing but an aggregate of autonomous individuals united together merely by an agreement of their own choosing. Inasmuch as coercion always involves a 'conflict' in the social behavior of the participants, then, for Marx, the social actions (of the participants) are to be seen as a function of their socially determined roles as actions of members of a certain socioeconomic class.[14] They are not the result of autonomous choice based on enlightened self-interest. Thus, coercive social relations and actions are explainable on the grounds of essentially institutionalized conflicts of social class, playing themselves out on the level of social behavior.

Marx replaces "the individual" of traditional individualism with a concept of a social being whose essence is defined by and not apart from society. Persons are defined by the type of productive activity they perform. He posits the view that "human nature" is modified and molded by the various phases of productive activity and historical development. Since the dominant forms of coercion are institutional and class related, Marx's vision of the ideal society is one where classes and the conflicts to which they give rise cease to exist, and coercive social institutions are obsolete.[15] In the classless society, exploitation and alienation are no longer necessary for the preservation of class interests.

Marx's philosophy, along with those of his predecessors Hegel and Feuerbach, represent a major turning point in the nineteenth century for philosophies rejecting earlier forms of abstract individualism.

J.S. Mill (1806-1873)

A contemporary of Marx's, J.S. Mill, perhaps the most well known of the nineteenth century libertarians, stands as the leading theorist of his period of the idea of individualism. For our purposes, what is most of interest in Mill's philosophy is his transition from a 'laissez-faire' individualism to a social individualism.

Mill's early individualism is so nicely summed up in his claim about autonomy: "There is a circle around every individual human being which no government . . . ought to be permitted to overstep."[16] His later social individualism evolved with his increasing emphasis upon gradually reforming social conditions in order to preserve and enrich true individuality in the context of society.

Mill's social individualism concentrated upon a person's social needs and so formed the basis for his argument for greater governmental involvement. Thus, he says, true individuality is best served when society helps to educate, and not neglect, individuals. In other words, general utility now encourages a greater degree of legitimate interference in the private affairs of individuals. In addition, the boundaries of the realm of privacy or autonomy have shifted.

Mill's concept of social autonomy is modified from his earlier to his later view of the individual. Any interference in the realm of individual privacy and self-development was undue and under certain conditions, coercive; but what changed was the realm he regarded as "private." Hence, if what was 'purely private' is really 'social', then no interference (e.g., coercion) occurs when a person is, for example, compelled into discharging an important social obligation or subdued into accepting social responsibility. For example, the case for and against paternal government in Mill's writings parallels the conceptual transition in his ideology of individualism in defining the limits of interference, justified interference, and noninterference in the promotion of those who reject the assistance.

A THREEFOLD CLASSIFICATION SCHEME OF PERSONHOOD, SOCIAL RELATIONS, AND HUMAN AUTONOMY

There are at least three distinct conceptions of personhood discernible in the philosophers' writings dealt with above. In turn these may also serve as criteria for the classification of the ideological conceptions behind some contemporary views of coercion. I use the term 'human' instead of 'individual' because the latter has a special bias for Western liberal social theory. 'Human' will receive appropriate modifications corresponding to the type of idea being discussed.

The first conception is the *abstract* or *solitary human*. It is most recognizable as the "atomic individual" of classical Liberalism. It is a view of the self-contained isolated 'private' person whose social relations ultimately resolve into its 'private' abstract constituents ('atomic' individuals). The philosophies of Hobbes, Locke, Kant, and the earlier writings of Mill are to be associated with this conception of personhood.

The second concept of personhood is the *social human* and belongs to treatments of 'persons' in the democratic and later, social phase of liberal theory. Behind this notion is the acknowledgment of social conditions and certain social relations vital to the person's self-constitution and self-fulfillment. This view stems primarily from the confluence in nineteenth century political theory of the currents of democracy and liberalism. It is from Mill's later idea of the "social individual" that the impact on welfare state liberal philosophers, from L. T. Hobhouse to John Dewey, is traceable. The third conception is the *community human*, which indicates that self-identity is inseparable from participation in a certain community. The modes of nonindividualism which we subsume under this conception are mainly characteristic of social theorists from Soviet Bloc and so-called Third World cultures. For instance, the Marxist (Soviet) idea of personhood is expressible as the "socialist personality," over and beyond "man, the producer" notion as the basic *human* attribute.[17]

Indeed, cultural anthropology and philosophy have shown that each culture holds certain implicit beliefs about the nature of the world and society as well as about perceptions that forge experience. Thus, in very different cultures, the experiences of people are often different from ours. To some degree, this also suggests that consciousness is a social formation. Therefore, to expect notions of personhood and autonomy, and thence, coercion, to vary from culture to culture is not unreasonable.

SOME CONTEMPORARY ANALYSES OF COERCION CLASSIFIED ACCORDING TO OUR CRITERIA OF INDIVIDUALISM AND NONINDIVIDUALISM

Because we in Western culture are so accustomed to viewing persons and relations individualistically, it is not always immediately apparent how profound the impact of this view is upon such concepts as human rights, freedom, autonomy, and coercion. The views below were selected as representative of the literature of its type in most contemporary analyses of coercion.

Some 'Solitary Human' Views of Coercion

These views place great emphasis on the 'private' individual and on relations between such private individuals. Following the writings of Kant and the early Mill, they hold that the essence of life is 'free individuality'. Their notion of internal subjective freedom (of individuality) is at the heart of the view of coercion.

Joel Feinberg discusses coercion in terms of "free individuality" as being the most valuable factor in the idea of taking moral responsibility in interpersonal relations.[18] For Feinberg, a basic presupposition of the good life is a vision of noninterference in the prior 'freedom of the individual'. Thus, he argues that (coercive) interference with an individual's basic freedom typically results in some important loss. So, the initial presumption should generally be in favor of the freedom of the individual.

A variation of this same presupposition is found in the work of H.L.A. Hart where he talks about coercion in connection with (interpersonal) moral and legal relations but also begins with a presumption in favor of individual freedom.[19] His view is that coercion is interference with freedom so that coercive interference always carries a greater burden of justification (unless morality itself is being coercively enforced.)

Others who write from the perspective of (the concept of) the private, abstract individual will emphasize certain personal, subjective (human) features or capacities in addition to the quality of 'free individuality'. For instance, some consider the question of coercion from the standpoint of the individual's possession of human rights. As such, these rights are basic features of the solitary human, the inviolable domain of his or her subjectivity in relation to other rights-possessing individuals. Coercion, as discussed by Rodney Peffer within the framework of interpersonal relations, is viewed as an interference or violation by others in the individual's otherwise self-determined, free exercise of his or her basic subjective rights.[20]

Another writer stresses 'reason' in an understanding of coercion.

Robert Paul Wolff claims that the power of reason permits its human possessor to assume complete responsibility for the choices he or she makes. Thus reason, in combination with freedom, makes each solitary individual subject only to his or her own will and morally obliged to refuse subjection to the will of others. Therefore, coercion treats individual persons as things controlled by causes instead of as beings instructed by 'reason'.[21]

The last set of writers I shall mention in this vein focusses on individual consent and privacy as the basis of the concept of the solitary human. According to one view, participants in a coercive event are described as individuals where the coercer imposes his or her private will upon that of another without or against his or her consent.[22] The claim is that individual consent is the sole ground of the intelligibility of 'coercion'.

Some writers consider individual privacy or domains of privacy to be central to coercion. In coercion, interpersonal relations are essentially social links between abstractly private subjects. Each subject is presumed to have an autonomous sphere of private space in which he or she is free to determine his or her own plans. Thus, coercion occurs when the private actions of a subject are either constrained or compelled by another or when the subject is denied self-control over his or her own sphere.[23]

Some 'Social Human' Views of Coercion

The following presentations are closely related to the *social* individualism found in Mill's later writings.

There is a serious social, nonindividualistic element in Douglas Husak's consideration of paternalism, coercion, and autonomy. It involves an identification of autonomy in terms of how circumstances actually influence a person's autonomy. It rejects outright the deontological presumption of abstract individual moral autonomy. Thus, he claims that some paternalistic forms of interference are noncoercive because they leave the subject's autonomy untouched or even promote it.[24] (Other writers usually regard paternalism per se as coercive, and question only its justification in certain circumstances.)

Thomas Scanlon focusses his analysis on the level of the *possible courses of social action* that the coercee considers as open to his or her self-expression. This is the basis for his discussion of the relationship between autonomy and coercion (and not merely of some supposed inviolable, fixed sphere of autonomy). Scanlon argues that coercion and autonomy may be compatible. For, if coercion entails restrictions on the capacity to choose (and not simply about the level of available choices), then the nonindividualistic element in Scanlon's view consists in the factor of the external, social manipulation of considerations and the supply of information regulating the available choices to the subject, which is imposed according to the plan of the coercing agent.[25]

Some 'Community Human' Views of Coercion

Various modes of nonindividualism are evident in the following cases in which coercive relations are construed in terms of members of groups or of social and political units and not as relations between abstract individuals who possess an a priori, fixed realm of personal or social autonomy between mere individuals with social needs.

Certain criteria are useful in identifying some treatments of coercion stressing nonindividualistic factors: (1) emphasis on the external, nonsubjective features of the concept of a 'public person;' (2) stress on society, the social unit, or its facets as the source of human self-identify; (3) emphasis on transcendental metaphysics or theological principles (or entities) as sources of identity (especially where a state, government, or some other social unit is understood as an expression of transcendental reality); (4) participants in the coercive event are interpreted as essentially members of a social or political unit. A particular conception of personhood may meet any or all these criteria.

B. F. Skinner (1904-   )

The view of B. F. Skinner seems to meet the first criterion. He makes no appeal in his view of coercion to a free, inner person who independently decides (not) to take certain actions. Indeed, Skinner calls this common notion "pre-scientific" because, in fact, there are no such things as undetermined choices, decisions, and final causes.

In his view there is no equation between coercion and control because all behavior is controlled (i.e., a set of responses to causes which are external to the individual). Coerced behavior occurs in the use of control techniques against the purposes of the controllee as expressed in the controller's actions or nonactions.

Skinner's version of a scientific view of behavior calls for the abolition of a "conception of the individual as doer, as an originator of action." He believes it is perfectly natural to resist selfish control, i.e., control exercised for the controller's selfish purposes. If 'control' means to influence, change, or shape human behavior, then, since all behavior is controlled, the philosophical dispute is not between freedom/autonomy vs. control but rather between scientifically controlled freedom/autonomy and unplanned, capricious control. In regards to the question of good government, the issue concerns not how freedom/autonomy can be preserved but what kind of controls are to be used and to what purpose.[26] To combat the dangers of aversive control for selfish purposes, Skinner recommends 'counter-controls' not the absence of controls.

A particularly repugnant, extreme biocultural, race-centered metaphysics (not too unlike the Nazi ideology) is illustrated in the general outlook of the South African Apartheid (by South African law, a strict separation of the races) theorists. The individual, group consciousness, and relations between different 'bio-cultural historical communities' constitute the basis of the self-concept of society in Apartheid philosophy.

The individual is conceived as an organic member of the community, while the community itself is believed to be a "biocultural volk organism." This is a collectivist idea of the self and suggests that the individual's home and community are the most significant spiritual aspect of life. Self-fulfillment is possible only inside the unified organism of the individual's own culture and society.[27]

In Apartheid theory, individuals are viewed from a 'group perspective'. Groups and communities are personified or invested with their own personalities, and these are assigned supreme intrinsic work. Difficulties arise, however, between different self-conscious groups because they see one another as threats. The uppermost duty of each member of a group is to safeguard the identity of his or her people against alienation, since it contains a spiritual treasure that has been entrusted to the living of the community. This is a clear rejection of Western liberal ideology which sees the individual as a 'moral sovereign'.

The Apartheid theorist sees it as his or her duty to exercise an uplifting (paternalistic) 'guardianship' over less self-conscious, retarded 'biocultural entities'. This special calling has become a racial political policy (Apartheid) for protecting the identity and integrity of the spiritual community of the Afrikaner and a solving of the 'race problem'. Apartheid theorists believe that "only groups that have attained 'volkish maturity' and cultural and technical sophistication requisite to the twentieth century can fully exercise self-determinantion."[28] Exogenous groups (like the Coloured and the Bantu) must be uplifted as a whole and never as individual members because this, it is believed, would alienate, dislocate, and uproot the individual.

The "guardianship" notion has an implication for the concept of coercion inasmuch as the worth of a group's self-expression depends upon the level of "volkish maturity"; less mature "volk" evidently are less worthy of self-expression. The burden of justification for the coercive imposition by the "mature" upon the "less developed volk" is held to fall, not on those who fail to gain the consent of the 'coercees', but on the 'coercees' who do not live within or work towards the "inner aims" of their spiritual community.

Thus, what is important in understanding coercion between groups is not 'consent' but the inability of the subdued group members to grasp the nature of his or her inherent volkish interests. Presumably these will determine the range of social autonomy the group has with respect to other communities. In short, coercion consists either in the purposeful denial of the self-realization of a community (or any of its members) or in the (noncoercive) "paternal" regulation of recalcitrants or deviants or "less developed" exogenous groups and individuals.

Ethnic Societies

In recent years we have witnessed the strategies of coercion of many ethnic-inspired acts of violence concerning threats and other hostilities towards ethnic groups. Coercion becomes perceived as a

legitimate form of ethnic self-expression when the group is denied
fulfillment as perceived by the group and when fulfillment means
the promise of human betterment. In effect coercion loses its
pejorative meaning, if not its character, as it is viewed as the
instrument of ethnic liberation. In writing about parallel situations
in both class-dominated and colonial societies, Jean-Paul Sartre
(and others like Albert Memmi and Franz Fanon) has claimed in
this vein that human freedom can only express itself as a "dialectic
of violence." It is through violence and coercion that oppressed
groups recreate their humanity and so work out some basic
freedom.[29]

In the formulation of public policy, many nation-states must
heed the growing political awareness for self-determination and
autonomy among their various indigenous ethnic groups. Indeed,
ethnic ideals often compete with national state ideals in the value
systems of ethnic groups. "Neoethnic behavior" resembles the
tribalism in less developed countries and is plaguing both Liberal
and Marxist societies.[30] For instance, we cite the Kurds of Iraq,
Ugandan tribal rivalries, Armenians in the Soviet Union, the
Montagnards in the south of Viet Nam, and the Basques in Spain,
to name but a few.

The last nonindividualist view I will mention has a certain
theological metaphysics behind its concept of human self-identity.
That is, the state of government or social units are understood as
manifestations of a transcendental reality. Individuals receive
whatever autonomy, freedom, and obligations they have from their
role as members of the social unit.

Coercion, as interpreted by some Islamic writers, is understood
in the context of the basically God-centered Islamic Republic. The
role of the state is to meet its obligation to enforce the supreme
principles of Islamic law (Shariah). Sovereignty is an Islamic
concept but only in regards to the state's relation to God:
sovereignty belongs only to God. Both rulers and ruled are under
obligation to promote God's will.

The earth-bound agents of divine authority claim to meet
peoples' religious needs by compelling conformity to divine law
and by penalizing those who violate or hinder conformity. This is
not seen as coercion in the usual pejorative Western liberal sense
because the sanctity of individual autonomy and freedom is not
construed in the same abstract manner. Religious values are basic

and "must prevail against all other values and considerations." "Individuals" are essentially members of the religious Islamic community. Though Islamic authority cannot compel persons to believe or have faith in God, it nevertheless certifies that those who do not forsake "the path of peace, security, beneficence and progress, and puts his moral and spiritual welfare in jeopardy." On the other hand, Islam "forbids cooperation in sin and transgression."[31]

In the 'community human' conception, generally, coercion is shaped by group membership and the ideals of the group, and not by relations between abstract individuals whose autonomy is determined and fixed prior to social relations.

SUMMARY OF THE CORRELATION BETWEEN IDEOLOGICAL CONCEPTS OF PERSONHOOD AND SOCIAL AUTONOMY, AND THE RELATIONAL VIEW OF COERCION

In the foregoing sections we have examined basic differences in conceptions of personhood. These have been identified as 'ideological' because within their respective traditions and contexts, the holders or believers of these concepts define, perceive, and interpret their social and political realities in terms of them. Along with differences in 'personhood' is a correlation with essential differences in the spheres of autonomy that have been attributed to 'persons.' Inasmuch as coercion is a power relation involving the coercer's control and diminishment of the victim's autonomy in his or her social (role) relation to the coercer, conceptual differences in the relative and shifting spheres of autonomy have been shown to affect both the nature and meaning of coercion. Therefore, the idea of coercion must be seen to some extent as being in part both a product and conceptual instrument of ideology.

Suppose each of us is a wholly autonomous individual ('solitary human') because of our possession of a free rational will (or, e.g., the capacity to make choices, and so on). As others bring pressure to bear upon us and so bend our reluctant or resisting will to theirs, we thereby lose our social autonomy to the others because they exercise coercive control over us in that respect.

On the other hand, let us suppose that our social autonomy is defined, not in separation and distinctness from others, but in our essential connectedness to a community. Our personhood originates and is fulfilled in our proper relationship to the social totality. Hence, the more we separate or define ourselves or our autonomy in disconnection from our community, the less of a human person we, as subjects, become. Consequently, coercive control means something different, and is exercised differently, from what it would be in the 'solitary human' ideology above. In short, one is coerced to the degree that the coercer diminishes the subject's social autonomy by distancing him or her from his or her community bond. Coercion is not simply a matter of 'forcing an unwilling will', but, rather, it involves the destruction of the victim's social autonomy as a 'community human'.

The sense of individuality for the subject is different in that neither the individual's will nor his or her autonomy is his or her own in the same way it is for the 'solitary human' individual. The closer the 'community human' is to the individual's community, the greater is his or her freedom and autonomy. Basic to the concept of coercion, then, is the phenomenon of distancing the subject from the community.

In conclusion, we recall that coercion should be analyzed as a four-term relation involving the elemental categories of participants, actions, instruments, and social roles.

TWO EXAMPLES OF IDEOLOGY-DEFINED COERCION: THE SLAVE SOCIETY AND RUSSIAN "REFUSENIKS"

An essential feature of a 'slave' society that distinguishes it from a non-slave society is the social status and manner of conceiving of its 'slaves'. In general, slaves have no officially recognized social autonomy. In this sense, then, slaves cannot be coerced. Like other 'non-human' or 'less-than-human' life forms, slaves are subdued or forced to do their master's bidding, but, in our strict sense of the term, they cannot be coerced. In reaching this conclusion, an ideological concept of the slave's 'personhood' is crucial.

However, a society that rejects slavery would likely see it as institutionalized violence and coercion; it is the relationship between master and slave that is coercive. Accordingly, although a master may treat his or her slave kindly, the relationship is nevertheless coercive in spite of the singular acts that are noncoercive in themselves.

Russian "Refuseniks" are Jewish people in contemporary Russia whose applications for exit visas due to religious persecution by the Soviet authorities have been denied. It is our typical view in the West that the 'Refuseniks' are coerced to stay in Russia because we believe they have the basic or prior human autonomy (as defined by our concept of natural human rights) to leave, which the Soviet government abridges (or coercively controls) by denying them exit visas.

The Soviets, on the other hand, do not regard Jews as having a basic human right to emigrate from Russia or a corresponding social autonomy because the 'community human' idea of the 'socialist personality' behind Soviet policy entails a supreme obligation to stay and fulfill one's duties to society and one's essential self. In short, leaving, for Jews, is not within the citizen's sphere of autonomy. Again, as in the paradigm slave society, non-socialist personalities (including those who ostensibly abdicate their personalities) have no social autonomy and so cannot be coerced. In contrast to our view, the plight of the Russian "Refuseniks" is seen differently.

NOTES

1. Michael A. Weinstein, "Coercion, Space and the Orders of Human Domination," in *Coercion: NOMOS XIV*, J. R. Pennock and J. W. Chapman, eds. (Chicago: Aldine-Atherton, 1972), pp. 64-65.

2. Yi-Fu Tuan, *Segmented Worlds and Self* (Minneapolis: University of Minnesota Press, 1982), pp. 151, 145, 166.

3. Ernst Cassirer, *The Myth of the State* (Garden City, N.Y.: Doubleday, 1955), pp. 38, 47; John Dewey and James Tufts, *Ethics* (New York: H. Holt and Co., 1938), p. 111.

4. Hannah Arendt, *The Human Condition* (Garden City, N.Y.: Anchor Books, 1959), pp. 35, 42; see also, Hannah Arendt, "What Was Authority?" in *Authority*, C. J. Friedrich, ed. (Cambridge, Mass.: Harvard University Press, 1958), p. 87, n5.

5. *The Republic of Plato,* F. M. Cornford, tr. (New York: Oxford University Press, 1964), pp. 142-43, 302-4, 306, 317. Plato, *Laws,* in *The Dialogues of Plato,* vol. 2, B. Jowett, tr. (New York: Random House,

1937), p. 563; Aristotle, *Politica,* in *The Basic Works of Aristotle,* Richard
McKeon, ed. (New York: Random House, 1941), p. 1217. Plato, *The
Statesman* in *The Dialogues of Plato,* vol. 2, p. 324; Plato, *Laws,* pp.
601-2. Aristotle, *Rhetoric,* in *The Basic Works of Aristotle,* p. 1361.
    6. Seneca, *De Beneficiis,* 3. 20, Aubrey Stewart, tr. (London: G. Bell
and Sons, 1900), p. 69; *The Communings with Himself of M. Aurelius
Antoninus,* 2. 13. 17, C. R. Haines, tr. (Cambridge, Mass.: Loeb Classical
Library, 1916), pp. 37, 41.
    7. Thomas Aquinas, *Summa Theologica,* vol. 1. (Cambridge:
Blackfriars, 1964) 1a. 2ae. quae. 91. art. 1 & 2; Walter Ullmann, *The
Individual and Society in the Middle Ages* (London: Methuen, 1967);
William S. Sahakian, *Systems of Ethics and Value Theory* (Totowa, N. J.:
Littlefield, Adams, 1968), p. 225; A. C. Pegis, ed., *Introduction to St.
Thomas Aquinas* (New York: The Modern Library, 1948), pp. 491-504;
Thomas Aquinas, *Summa Theologica* Vol. 1 (Cambridge: Blackfriars,
1964), quae. 6. art. 4.
    8. T. Hobbes, *Leviathan,* vol. 1 (New York: Bobbs-Merrill, 1958), pp.
106-9, 120, 124, 142.
    9. John Locke, *The Treatises of Government,* 2d edition (Cambridge:
Cambridge University Press, 1967), pp. 95, 99.
    10. Jean Jacques Rousseau, *The Social Contract and Discourse on the
Origin of Equality,* L. Crocker, ed. (New York: Washington Square Press,
1967), pp. 27, 181, 201, 212, 214.
    11. *Kant: The Moral Law,* H. J. Paton, tr. (London: Hutchinson, 1956),
pp. 95-96; Immanuel Kant, *Fundamental Principles of the Metaphysics of
Morals,* T. K. Abbott, tr. (Indianapolis: Bobbs-Merrill, 1975), p. 50;
Immanuel Kant, "Theory and Practice," in *Kant's Political Writings,* H.
Reiss, ed. (New York: Cambridge University Press, 1970), pp. 74, 137, 163.
    12. G. W. F. Hegel, *The Philosophy of Right,* T. M. Knox, tr. (New
York: Oxford University Press, 1973), sec. 260, p. 348; sec. 144(3), pp. x,
365; sec. 270(10); secs. 15, 29, 92; secs. 344, 448; sec. 1060, pp. xi, 334; sec.
91. See Manfred Reidel, in *Hegel's Political Philosophy,* Z. A. Pelczynski,
ed. (Cambridge: Cambridge University Press, 1971), p. 7. G.W.F. Hegel,
National Law, T. M. Knox, tr. (Philadelphia: University of Pennsylvania
Press, 1975), pp. 128, 119, 17, 89, 88, 91.
    13. For example, Karl Marx, *The Economic and Philosophic
Manuscripts of 1844*, Dirk Struik, ed. (New York: International
Publishers, 1964), p. 146; also Karl Marx, *The Poverty of Philosophy* (New
York: International Publishers, 1963), p. 174.
    14. Karl Marx and Friederich Engels, *The German Ideology*, R. Pascal,
ed. (New York: International Publishers, 1966), p. 76.
    15. Marx, *Economic and Philosophic Manuscripts,* pp. 102-3; Karl
Marx, *Capital,* vol. 1 (New York: International Publishers, 1967), pp. 609,
183-84; Karl Marx, *Grundrisse,* Martin Nicolaus, tr. (New York: Vintage

Books, 1973), p. 84; Karl Marx, *Civil War in France* (New York: International Publishers, 1940), pp. 54-58 and passim; and Karl Marx, *Class Struggles in France 1848-1850* (New York: International Publishers, 1964), pp. 126 and passim.

16. J. S. Mill, "On Liberty," in *The Utilitarians* (New York: Dolphin Books, 1961), pp. 532, 552; J. S. Mill, *Principles of Political Economy*, D. Winch, ed. (New York: Penguin Books, 1970), p. 306; also "The Claims of Labor," in J. S. Mill, *Essays on Economics and Society*, vol. 4, J. M. Robson, ed. (Toronto: University of Toronto Press, 1967), pp. 379-80.

17. Alan Rosenbaum, "On the Philosophical Foundations of the Conception of Human Rights," *Philosophy Research Archives* (March 1985); also, see the text, especially Article 39, of the "Constitution (Fundamental Law) of the Union of Soviet Socialist Republics," adopted October 7, 1977, in *Great Soviet Encyclopedia,* vol. 31, trans. of 3rd edition (New York: Macmillan, 1982).

18. Joel Feinberg, *Social Philosophy* (Englewood Cliffs, N. J.: Prentice-Hall, 1973); also see Martin Golding, *Philosophy of Law* (Englewood Cliffs, N. J.: Prentice-Hall, 1975).

19. H. L. A. Hart, *Law, Liberty, and Morality* (Stanford, Calif.: Stanford University Press, 1963), pp. 5-6, 31-33, 46, 76-77, 82-83.

20. Rodney Peffer, *Philosophy and Public Affairs* 8, 1 (Fall 1978), pp. 65-66, 77.

21. Robert Paul Wolff, *In Defense of Anarchism* (New York: Harper & Row, 1970), pp. 12-14, 18; and R. P. Wolff, "Is Coercion 'Ethically Neutral'?" in *Coercion,* Pennock and Chapman, eds., p. 146.

22. Bernard Dauenhauer, "Politics and Coercion," in *Philosophy Today* (July 1978).

23. For example, see Hans Kelsen, *General Theory of Law and State* (New York: Russell & Russell, 1961), pp. 18, 99-103, 107-8, 303-5, and also B. Bandman and E. Bandman, "Coercion vs. Freedom," in *Bioethics and Human Rights* (Boston: Little, Brown, 1978), p. 149-53; and Bernard Gert and C. Culver, "Paternalistic Behavior," *Philosophy and Public Affairs* 6, 1 (Fall 1976), p. 46.

24. Douglas Husak, "Paternalism and Autonomy," *Philosophy and Public Affairs* 10, 1 (Winter 1981), pp. 27-46.

25. See Thomas Scanlon, "A Theory of Freedom of Expression," in *Philosophy of Law,* Ronald M. Dworkin, ed. (New York: Oxford University Press, 1977), p. 163.

26. B. F. Skinner, *Science and Human Behavior* (New York: Free Press, 1965), pp. 30-31, 285, 447-48, 592, 594-95; Melvin Rader, *The Enduring Questions* (New York: Holt, Rinehart and Winston, 1950), p. 606.

27. A. J. Gregor, *Contemporary Ideologies* (New York: Random House, 1968), pp. 244, 237, 254.

28. J. K. Ngubane, *An African Explains Apartheid* (New York: Praeger,

1963), p. 12. A. B. Du Preez, *Inside the South African Crucible* (Kaapstad, South Africa: H.A.U.M., 1959) pp. 56, 86, 89, 118-19, 121; see also G. Carter, *The Politics of Inequality* (London: Thames and Hudson, 1954), p. 273.

29. See Jean-Paul Sartre, *Critique of Dialectical Reason,* A. Sheridan-Smith, tr. (London: NLB, 1978), p. 736.

30. A. A. Said and L. R. Simmons, eds. *Ethnicity in an International Context* (New Brunswick, N. J.: Transaction, 1976), pp. 35-37.

31. M. Zafrulla Khan, *Islam and Human Rights* (London: Ascot Press, 1976), pp. 123, 79, 82, 146, 192, 116.

Selected Bibliography and Suggested Further Readings

Berlin, Isaiah. *Four Essays on Liberty* (New York: Oxford University Press, 1979).

Dworkin, Ronald M., ed. *Philosophy of Law* (New York: Oxford University Press, 1977).

Feinberg, Joel. *Social Philosophy* (Englewood Cliffs, N.J.: Prentice-Hall, 1973).

Hampshire, Stuart, ed. *Public and Private Morality* (New York: Cambridge University Press, 1979).

Hart, H.L.A. *Law, Liberty and Morality* (Stanford, Calif.: Stanford University Press, 1963).

Honderich, Ted, ed. *Essays on Freedom of Action* (London: Routledge & Kegan Paul, 1973).

Keat, Russell, and Urry, John. *Social Theory as Science,* 2d edition (Boston: Routledge & Kegan Paul, 1982).

Mill, J. S. "On Liberty," *The Utilitarians* (New York: Dolphin Books, 1961).

Oppenheim, Felix. *The Dimensions of Freedom* (New York: St. Martin's Press, 1970).

Patterson, Orlando. *Slavery and Social Death* (Cambridge, Mass.: Harvard University Press, 1982).

Pennock, J. R., and Chapman, J. W., eds. *Coercion: NOMOS XIV* (Chicago: Aldine-Atherton Press, 1972).

Schutz, Alfred. *Collected Papers,* vol. 2 (The Hague, Netherlands: Martinus Nijhoff, 1964).

ARTICLES

Alexander, Lawrence. "Zimmerman on Coercive Wage Offers." *Philosophy and Public Affairs* 12 (Spring 1983).

Benn, S. I. "Freedom, Autonomy, and the Concept of a Person." *Proceedings of the Aristotelian Society* 76 (1975-76).

188   Selected Bibliography and Suggested Further Readings

Dauenhauer, Bernard. "Politics and Coercion." *Philosophy Today* (July 1978).
DeGeorge, Richard. "Social Reality and Social Relations." *Review of Metaphysics* 37 (September 1983).
Fowler, Mark. "Coercion and Practical Reason." *Social Theory and Practice* 8, 3 (Fall 1982).
Gunderson, Martin. "Threats of Coercion." *Canadian Journal of Philosophy* 9, 2 (June 1979).
Husak, Douglas. "Paternalism and Autonomy." *Philosophy and Public Affairs* 10, 1 (Winter 1981).
Kuflik, Arthur. "The Inalienability of Autonomy." *Philosophy and Public Affairs* 13, 4 (Fall 1984).
McCloskey, H. J. "Coercion: Its Nature and Significance." *Southern Journal of Philosophy* (Fall 1980).
Oppenheim, Felix. "'Constraints on Freedom' as a Descriptive Concept." *Ethics* 95 (January 1985).
Philips, Michael. "Are Coerced Agreements Involuntary?" *Law and Philosophy* 3 (1984).
Ryan, Cheney. "The Normative Concept of Coercion." *Mind* 89 (October 1980).
Sankowski, Edward. "'Paternalism' and Social Policy." *American Philosophical Quarterly* 22, 1 (January 1985).
Sen, Amartya. "Freedom and Agency." *The Journal of Philosophy* 82, 4 (April 1985).
Teichman, Jenny. "The Definition of *Person*." *Philosophy* 60, 232 (April 1985).
Wilson, Patrick. "Ryan on Coercion." *Mind* 91 (April 1982).
Young, Robert. "Autonomy and Paternalism." *Canadian Journal of Philosophy,* supp. vol. 8 (1982).

Index

About the Author

ALAN S. ROSENBAUM, Associate Professor of Philosophy at
Cleveland State University, has written extensively in the areas of
human rights and legal philosophy. Among his earlier publications
is *The Philosophy of Human Rights* (Greenwood Press, 1980).

3 5282 00109 6661